THE
NOVEL
ENTREPRENEUR
A HEART-CENTERED PATH FOR FULFILLMENT

THE NOVEL ENTREPRENEUR
A HEART-CENTERED PATH FOR FULFILLMENT

SALLY BENDERSKY

The Novel Entrepreneur

A Heart-Centered Path for Fulfillment

Copyright © 2017, Sally Bendersky

The views expressed by the author in reference to specific people in their book represent entirely their own individual opinions and are not in any way reflective of the views of Transformation Catalyst Books, LLC. We assume no responsibility for errors, omissions, or contradictory interpretation of the subject matter herein.

Transformation Catalyst Books, LLC does not warrant the performance, effectiveness, or applicability of any websites listed in or linked to this publication. The purchaser or reader of this publication assumes responsibility of the use of these materials and information. Transformation Catalyst Books, LLC shall in no event be held liable to any party for any direct, indirect, punitive, special, incidental, or any other consequential damages arising directly or indirectly from any use of this material. Techniques and processes given in this book are not to be used in place of medical or other professional advice.

No part of this book may be reproduced or transmitted in any form, or by any means, electronic or mechanical, including photography, recording, or in any information storage or retrieval system without written permission from the author or publisher, except in the case of brief quotations embodied in articles and reviews.

Published by:
Transformation Books
211 Pauline Drive #513
York, PA 17402
www.TransformationBooks.com

ISBN: 978-1-945252-31-0
Library of Congress Control Number: 2017956152

Cover design: Ranilo Cabo
Layout and typesetting: Ranilo Cabo
Editor: Michelle Cohen
Proofreader: Gwen Hoffnagle
Book Midwife: Carrie Jareed

Printed in the United States of America

This book is dedicated to my most beloved women and men of the future:
Benjamin, Maya, Antonia, Jeremy, Gabriel, Naomi, and Arthur

TABLE OF CONTENTS

Foreword 1
Introduction 7

Chapter 1	Starting from the Beginning 15	
	Early Years 15	
	My Early Years 16	
	Now It's Your Turn 25	
Chapter 2	Facts and Interpretations............................29	
Chapter 3	Is Your Glass Half Empty or Half Full? 39	
Chapter 4	How You See Yourself: Strengths and Weaknesses 51	
Chapter 5	The Observers That You Are 59	
	Are You One and Only? 59	
	Context and Observers 60	
	The Observer Who Observes the Observer 62	
Chapter 6	Your Divine Gifts 69	
	Receiving and Returning............................69	
	The Greatest Gift of All: Finding Meaning in Your Life......................75	

Chapter 7	**The Body-Emotion-Language Connection**	**81**
	Being and Acting	81
	Observing Yourself and Others in Action	83
	Aligning Body, Emotions, and Language in Conversations	88
Chapter 8	**Incubation of PEL-MET**	**93**
	What Your Body Can Show You	93
	The Role of Habits	98
	PEL-MET Is Born	98
	The Why, How, and What of PEL-MET	99
	Discovering PEL-MET through Experience	102
	Preparing Yourself for PEL-MET	103
Chapter 9	**Getting Ready for PEL-MET, Step 3**	**105**
	Connecting Body and Emotions	105
	Emotions, Feelings, and Moods	109
	PEL-MET, Step 3	115
Chapter 10	**PEL-MET Verbal Steps**	**117**
	Dreams and Desires; Purpose and Objectives	117
	PEL-MET, Step 4: Checking and Asking	121
	PEL-MET Step 5: Call for Action	124
	The Five Steps of PEL-MET	*126*
	PEL-MET Blueprint	127

Chapter 11	The Power of Conversations 131
	What Is Special about Human Language? 131
	Outcomes of Conversations 134
	The Basic Linguistic Actions in Conversations 138

Chapter 12	The Magic of Listening 141
	Solving the Mystery of Listening 141
	How You Can Improve Your Listening 147
	Opportunities that Listening Provides: Understanding and Transformation 151

Chapter 13	Creating New Realities through the Act of Speaking 155
	Two Modalities of Speaking: Proposal and Inquiry 155
	The Acts of Speech: Are You Describing or Creating Your World? 158

Chapter 14	A Special Kind of Declaration 169
	Declarations That Judge 169
	Assessments and Time 172
	Validation of Assessments 178
	Do Not Confuse Assertions with Assessments 183

Chapter 15	Coordination of Direct Action 189
	Requests and Offers 189
	Managing a Promise 200
	Do You Complain or Whine? 203

Chapter 16	Trust 209
	A Widely Used Term that Is Difficult to Define.....209
	Trust and Distrust 216
	The Impact of Forgiveness 220
	Trusting and Distrusting Organizational Cultures .. 222
	Building Self-Confidence 226

Chapter 17	Why the Latest Findings in Neuroscience Matter!..229
	Taking a Look at the Human Brain..........................229
	The New Science of Mind 233
	Brain's Action Affects Your Life 236
	Predominance of Bad over Good 239
	Consequences of Neuroplasticity 241
	The Neuroscience of Conversations 245
	Neuroscience beyond the Cephalic Brain: Your Heart and Gut 249

Chapter 18	The Novel Entrepreneur..255

Acknowledgments 261
About The Author 265

FOREWORD

This book is necessary. It's a book we have been waiting for, maybe without knowing, but when it comes into our hands we hear ourselves saying, "How timely!" I celebrate, therefore, its coming to light.

The Novel Entrepreneur has multiple merits. It expresses an invitation for the reader to reexamine their way of living from a different point of view to the one they possibly are used to having. This is a viewpoint that sustains itself on the importance of our conversations and on their power to shape our particular way of being, the relationships we establish with others, and the quality of our existence.

During the second half of last century, philosopher Martin Buber stated that human beings are conversational beings. He said that conversations lead us to be the way we are. This means that if our conversations change, our way of being will also change. Nevertheless, many years had to pass until we could fully understand what this meant. This is a book that allows us to appreciate Buber's statements. It is precisely an invitation to become who we want to be by means of altering the way we converse with others and with ourselves.

The great German philosopher Friedrich Nietzsche fervently instructs us: "Become who you are!" This means that it is necessary to acknowledge that who we are now is not an expression of who we really are. We are just sounding boards of past conversations, of manifestations that we repeat thinking they are ours; however, they are generally taken from our environment. The self that we are, the one that develops into our singularity, does not come from the past, but is waiting for us in the future. It is an "I" that is in front of us. It is an "I" that needs to be cultivated, pursued, and reached in order to substitute, step-by-step, the one we passively inherited.

Sally Bendersky leads the reader through each chapter into observing themselves from the perspective that Buber suggested, invites them to ask questions that will allow them to reach a more fulfilled life, and encourages them to dispel the problems that have troubled them until now. One of the great merits of *The Novel Entrepreneur* is that the reader might be surprised by their own self while they reach a more solid understanding of how they are. Within each step of this book, readers will discover a set of questions and exercises that will steadily transform them.

Interestingly, the reader who starts this book will not be the same as the reader who reaches the end of it. They will feel that they have taken a journey, even though they may never have left the comfort of their home. Each reader will be able to recognize that they have been relocated to a much deeper level, allowing them to observe things they were not able to see before, and, also, to make their usual observations from a different perspective. Their world will slowly have started to whirl until it will have turned into a different one.

This is a delicate book; it is not hasty, and it is committed to the reader. One perceives this immediately from its beginning. It is evident that what is important here is that the reader savors each of the statements exposed and makes the most of it for the benefit of their own life. In this sense, the book is surprisingly generous. Its main character is not the author, nor the rest of the characters mentioned by the author. The main character is actually the reader. It is true that while Sally tells us about her own life and the experiences of other people, she introduces us to ourselves while the reading progresses. The emphasis is always placed on the reader and on the possibility of their using what the book states in order to know themselves in a new way and to take responsibility for themselves in a better way. I often point out that this type of journey is the equivalent of crossing to the other side of the mirror only to discover, upon arrival, that one had been living on the wrong side.

Friedrich Nietzsche stated, "We, who know, are unknown to ourselves." This sentence can be read in multiple ways. On one hand, it cautions us on how little we know and understand ourselves. On the other hand, it guides us to penetrate deeply within to know ourselves better. Society provides education that teaches us many things, but usually its focus is placed on outside factors, away from our inner selves. Seldom do we come out of it knowing ourselves better.

And yet we will hardly find more important knowledge than that which allows us to dive inward and get to know ourselves better. All other knowledge should be supported by this single one. It was not in vain that ancient Greeks visited the Oracle of Delphos and asked Pythia, priestess of god Apollo, to clarify some mystery of what the future had in store. At the door of the Oracle they could find the written phrase "Know thyself," in anticipation of the reply they would later receive from her.

This was a central element of Greek wisdom, and we can see it in the statements of several of its philosophers. Heraclitus pointed out to us: "Your character is your destiny." How you are—your "character"—determines your future. From this phrase we can conclude that if you accomplish changing your way of being, you will end up altering what life has in store for you. This is also the main teaching of Socrates, the philosopher of the incessant questions, who invites us to undertake a permanent inquiry of ourselves and also warns us: "The unexamined life is not worth living."

But Nietzsche's statement also has a different and no less important meaning. It also posits that the knowledge of the human soul, of the particular way of being of each one of us, will never be fully and completely accomplished. Knowledge of the human soul is always limited. Its background is, and will always be, mysterious no matter how deeply we dig into it. Sally is careful not to make us believe otherwise, and this is also part of her sensitivity, which comes forth in her writing.

FOREWORD

The strength of this book does not only reside in its theoretical rigor, but also in its ability to translate concepts and distinctions into specific questions, committed to the transformational practice of the reader. This is a respectful book. It never instructs the reader on how to lead their life. It only makes an invitation to formulate questions, to offer personal answers, and to extract from them the corresponding conclusions. The reader's own conclusions will lead them to behave in a different way. Therefore, as we have already said, this is a book that allows us to see what we were not able to see before, and to take actions that previously we could not take.

In that sense, *The Novel Entrepreneur* claims that the value of questions is greater than that of answers and is a fundamental, ethical criterion to lead our lives. Those who live through answers are condemned to discover again and again that the answers wither and are useless. This has become a distinctive feature of our time. When that happens, we compromise the meaning of our lives, which fall into crises of greater or lesser magnitudes. On the other hand, those who live through questions will be able to get up on their feet every time they feel that the erosion suffered by their answers has led them into a vacuum. Today, humanity has no option but to transit from the value we gave to answers in the past to the value that questions offer us to cope with the future in a better way. This is a book that understands this principle.

That is why I invite the reader to dive into it and let yourself be carried away by the multiple challenges that await you. If there is something you can all be sure of, it is that the path will be different for everyone. It will be a tailored path for each reader's concerns and aspirations since—although led by the respectful hand of the author—each reader will have charted their own course.

Rafael Echeverría
President of Newfield Consulting Santiago, May 2016

INTRODUCTION

A couple of years ago I was watching a presentation by the late Dr. Wayne Dyer.[1] He and his presentation were full of energy and inspiration, although it was no mystery that he was severely ill. Dyer seemed at peace, fulfilled, and his passion was contagious even though I was watching and listening through my computer screen.

Suddenly I felt as if a strong blow had hit me when I heard him say,

"Don't die with the music still inside you!"

I could not wait a second longer.

To some extent I have had the privilege of sharing my music in my leadership and coaching practice. But at that moment I

---

1. http://www.drwaynedyer.com/about-dr-wayne-dyer

felt a sense of urgency, a profound desire to reach many more people. A voice inside me exclaimed, *It's time to write a book!*

I have personally experienced and have also been a witness to other people's astounding transformation and learning. I need to share it now. Why? Because I have no doubt that you will resonate with more than one of the melodies, rhythms, and harmonies that you will find in this book. I know you will discover important issues in regard to some of your unanswered questions. More important, you will ask new questions that will help you in your journey towards an exciting, joyous, loving, and fulfilled life.

In this book you will find new and adapted strategies, methods, and tools that cover the most essential aspects that will allow you to become the leader—the novel entrepreneur—of your own life. You will not only receive information and inspiration, but you will also be able to practice your new or renovated learning through a number of exercises. They will lead you to reaffirm yourself and your capacities in some aspects, and to open new ground in others. You will learn how to decide who you want to be and how you want to behave in contexts that matter to you, such as family, work, marriage, community involvement, and others.

Looking back, I date a leap in my awareness and the beginning of a deep emotional transformation to late 1986. At that time I was a divorced mother of two and an engineer working in banking information technology. I could not even imagine that fulfillment was possible for me. My professional goal was to earn enough money to raise my children. It was as

INTRODUCTION

much as I could possibly dream at that time. I was sure I would never get a promotion because of my gender, and boredom was a natural part of the game. To make things worse, I had a romantic relationship that was coming to an end and I felt very lonely, unloved, and maybe unlovable. I started developing a strong sense of victimhood and hopelessness.

In October of 1986, I went to a workshop that I now see as the point of ignition of a huge transformation in my awareness and my basic mood in life. The presenter offered his audience to increase their productivity and well-being in the course of three days. His way of showing new perspectives and of relating to the participants turned my usual behavior upside down. From a quiet introvert, I suddenly became a woman who was anxious to relate to other people and to communicate with them. I fell into an irresistible, huge, and marvelous new space, like Alice in Wonderland.

That experience changed my life. Less than five years later, in 1991, I was no longer working in information technology at a bank. I had finished my gestalt therapy training in Santiago, where I had become an organizational consultant, and was studying psychology at the university. I was living with my new—at the time—husband and heading to San Francisco to start my training as a coach.

Never again did I experience hopelessness or victimhood. From then on I developed a fascinating and ambitious career that allowed me to integrate many different sources of learning. The world became a wonderful place in which to live. The best part is that I gained a strong conviction that I had a great role to play in designing and developing the life I wanted. Actually, I learned how to dream and how to turn those dreams into viable projects.

Magically, what I learned helped me as well as others who wanted to transform themselves into who they longed to be. It was really a simultaneous process of learning and at the same time sharing with others, many of whom also learned and shared their insights.

If I was able to become the leader of my own life, I have no doubt that you will also accomplish it. *The Novel Entrpreneur* intends to show that you can dream, have a vision, and define your own purpose and goals for your life. You can also design the journey to meet your purpose and goals, and prepare yourself with the right help, tools, and equipment to make the journey, enjoy it, and travel as far as possible. In other words, you can adapt the circumstances to your dreams instead of passively adapting to the circumstances you find in your life.

You surely have more freedom to design and travel your path than you might be willing to acknowledge. However, it is not unlimited, precisely because of your conditioning, unconscious beliefs, and hidden emotions. You might not even be aware of them, but nevertheless they have the power to define boundaries for your possible actions and restrict your behaviors.

You can observe a human being simultaneously in three different dimensions. First, as a species, all human beings are alike. Second, some of us are similar to certain other people or groups of people and different from others. For example, women's bodies tend to be alike, and they are different from men's bodies. And third, every one of us is unique. Have you found someone who is identical in every possible aspect to someone else? You will not find this even in identical twins. Your personality and your soul are unique. Just think of what is possible when unique, creative souls get together to build something! And these particular souls belong to one single species and to several groups with similar features. These similarities act as anchors for mutual understanding. They help us build creative collectives.

The first two dimensions, human species and similarities and differences, allow us to feel that we belong. In exchange for that safe feeling, our behavior must conform to certain restrictions and expectations from the groups where we belong, inhibiting some of the freedom that our uniqueness might be inclined towards. This book provides you with tools and strategies for stretching the boundaries and restrictions created by conditioning, unconscious beliefs, and hidden emotions in order to expand your world of possibilities.

There is a crucial condition that enables you to expand your world: you must believe that you can make it happen. Unfortunately my personal experience with the vast majority of my clients, and particularly with women, has been an initial predisposition towards denial of their potential. It is as if they said, "I cannot and will not achieve a purpose, mission, or life goal. So what's the use of dreaming and thinking unrealistic big things?" Sometimes this powerlessness is clearly expressed, and at times it is concealed. But believe me, whether conscious or unconscious, the feeling of existing limitations is there and determines your possibilities in life.

I have come to the conclusion that the feeling of lack of power is part of gender conditioning in certain cultures. Although it is true that gender differences have been narrowing with time, there is still a limiting mindset, both in men and women, that changes very slowly. For example, empirical data from my working with hundreds of male and female coaching clients show that many men are reluctant to have a female boss. Female disempowerment and male reluctance, as unconscious as they might be, make a poisonous, stagnating combination.

If you believe in your capacity to make things happen, you will be proactive in dealing with your challenges. You will not feel and behave like a helpless victim in a world in which you have no power to create, build, or change it. On the contrary, you will feel responsible for your own life, you will dare to dream big, and you will look for the help you need in order to design your path, travel it, and face the obstacles that are inevitably waiting for you and which you will need to overcome.

Through this book I am inviting you to build, together with others, a world that is open to learning, while using and developing your divine resources, several of which you will discover in these pages. You will learn how to connect authentically to yourself and to other people. You will design a path that will lead you to be fulfilled by who you are and what you do with your life.

INTRODUCTION

I urge you to discover your own vision and to live according to it. This book is a reference guide for your journey. I invite you to travel with your whole being and the self-confidence you are entitled to. Do not allow yourself to be intimidated by the numerous threats, perils, and obstacles that you will surely encounter on this amazing path. This is YOUR journey. In spite of your probable limitations, you have huge potential for growth and self-development.

The Novel Entrepreneur offers specific guidelines that will shift your mindset into thinking big and discovering your purpose in life and in all the areas that are important to you. You will also find tools for identifying your limiting beliefs and overcoming them. You will learn how to deal with your feelings and emotions so that they help you in your journey instead of blocking your way. Finally, you will determine how to have the conversations you need in order to pave the road to your fulfillment.

Your journey begins with this book. I will be at your side, and we will walk step by step while you capture the information, live the experiences, reflect upon the stories, and take the first autonomous strides.

Enjoy the transformation that you are about to experience!

CHAPTER 1

Starting from the Beginning

Early Years

People have a huge capacity for learning, as you will see many times while reading this book.

One of the things you will learn is how your past experiences influence your present life and what influence the present might have on your future. Time can be considered a continuous line along which your life happens. If you are to design and travel a heart-centered path for fulfillment, it is imperative to learn as much as you can about yourself.

For this to happen you will need to go over your early years, since the younger a person is the more important the changes that take place in their life can be. A child grows under a multitude of influences that interact, produce an impact on their life, and somewhat determine the person they will become one day. These influences are genetic and environmental. Culture can have a huge impact on a child's development. Other factors including parenting styles, friends, teachers, and schools also play big roles, especially during the first five or six years of life.

Understanding your early years will help you, as an adult, determine what you want to reinforce from your initial learning in life and what you want to create or change. I invite you to look at my story of my early years, and then to take a peek at yours. This is the first station on the road to prepare you to live a fulfilled life.

My Early Years

Born in Santiago, Chile, I am a baby-boomer and daughter of an Argentinian father and a Romanian mother. (She was born in Romania, but by the time she arrived in Chile her city belonged to the Soviet Union and later on to Ukraine.) My father's parents had come to Argentina from Russia as children in a massive emigration that took place during the last decades of the nineteenth century. My grandmother was about fifteen years old when she married my grandfather in Argentina. I never met him because he fell ill and passed away many years before I was born. They had eight children, one of whom died as a baby. My father, who was born in 1917, arrived as a teenager in Chile in 1930. His elder sister took care of him. She had settled in Santiago, Chile, with her husband ten years earlier.

My mother arrived in Chile two years after the end of the World War II, in July of 1947, and didn't know anything about the place to which she had emigrated. She didn't speak a word of Spanish. My mother was still traumatized by having lived the years of World War II in deportation in a special place for Jews: Transnistria.

This was a barren place in Eastern Europe that had been conquered by the Germans and given by the Führer to his ally, the Romanian dictator Antonescu, in compensation for his loyalty. The Jews were taken by force to Transnistria with the intention of letting them die of hunger, typhoid fever, cold, and shootings. They were clearly not allowed to work, so they were not able to make a living.

My mother survived, but her mother, my grandmother to whom I owe my name, could not make it. She was fifty-two years old when she died in transit from one place of horror to another. When the war was over and the Soviets occupied the place, my mother returned home to find no one she knew there,[2] so she went to Bucharest, the capital of Romania, to stay at her sister's house. Because Romania had lost part of its territory after the war, including my mother's birthplace, Cernauti,[3] she lost her Romanian citizenship and became a non-entity, not officially allowed to live in Bucharest. She was

---
2. In the twenty-first century, after my mother had passed away, it became known that no more than 30% of the deportees to Transnistria survived.
3. This is the Romanian name of the city, but to this day Jews refer to it as Czernowitz, the name it had when it belonged to the Austro-Hungarian Empire until 1918. My mother was born in Romania four years later, in 1922.

denounced by a neighbor who heard her voice coming from my aunt's kitchen, and had to leave her sister's house. That is why my mother lived in hiding in Bucharest and joined a group of religious Jews (she was not) who were preparing the illegal smuggling of Jews into Palestine.

My mother went to Paris with her group, where they waited for the ship that would take them to Palestine. She had been in the city for two months when someone from a Jewish agency, with the mission of helping Jews find lost relatives, approached her. The man showed her a letter that had reached the Agency. It had been written by her brother, who was desperately trying to find her and their mother. He had asked the agency for help in securing them passage on a ship that would take them to the port of Valparaíso, Chile, where he had settled in the late thirties, thinking he would have the means to bring his mother and sister there in a couple of years. But the war had crushed his plans, and they lost contact for more than six years. That is why he did not know that his mother had died in terribly dire conditions. Finally my mother did what her brother wanted her to do and travelled to the opposite side of the world, contrary to her first intention of emigrating to Palestine.

I never knew, and my mother is not with us any more to ask her, if she was happy to change her plans of emigrating illegally to Palestine or if she did so because of a sense of family obligation. I do know that she revered her brother.

My father seems to have been a lively young man who worked hard on weekdays and enjoyed going to the mountain or the sea with a large group of friends, boys and girls, during weekends. I imagine it was in this group that he fell in love with a sweet, small young woman who was finishing her university studies, a rare deed for a woman at that time, and would soon become a pharmacist. (My father finished his studies when he was twelve years old.) Soon after they got married she became pregnant and delivered my elder half-brother after seven months of pregnancy. His mother died in childbirth. This happened in late November of 1945.

I have been told that my father spent months of great grief, from which it took him some years to recover. Apparently everyone agreed that he was not fit to take care of his premature newborn son by himself. Both families declared that they were the ones who were more suited to raise the child until my father could pick up the pieces of his life, and a certain tension started growing among my father's in-laws and his sisters. By now his whole family lived in Chile, and his father had died a decade before in Santiago, shortly after arriving from Argentina.

My mother arrived in Chile in July of 1947, and was very well received by her brother and his wife, although it was difficult for everyone to find something in common with her. My aunt hosted parties, and my mother hid in the kitchen. The couple had met my father socially, liked him, and was aware of the grief and the unstable situation in the upbringing of his child. Meetings were arranged here and there among all the families involved, and the young, suffering man was introduced to the war-traumatized young woman. Six months later they were married, although there still had to be a lot of nonverbal communication between them. My mother knew no Spanish, and my father spoke only that language and also a very basic, broken Yiddish, which was the language my mother used to talk with my grandmother back in Europe. By marrying my father she made the commitment to raise a two-year-old little boy before she had had the time to really settle herself, learn the language, and become immersed in the Chilean culture. My father's former mother-in-law treated my mother as if she were her own real, loving mother. She considered all of us, my mother's children, as her own grandchildren. Later, in my teens, she became my mentor in coping with the difficult facts of my life, one of which was precisely my mother.

When I was already an adult with grown children, my mother once told me that when she and my father got married they had a serious conversation in which they decided that they would wait some years before having another child. As things turned out, each of them thought the other would take the necessary precautions. The result of that misunderstanding was the birth of my twin brother and me, nine months after the wedding. My mother became the mother of three children only fourteen months after having arrived from a different world and the destruction of all that had been her previous life. They did wait almost four years before bringing my younger sister into this world.

We had a relatively comfortable life while we were children and youngsters. My father worked with my uncle, the one who had brought my mother to Chile. I think this uncle was obsessed with becoming a tycoon. He created several industrial factories, some of which still exist although they were sold many decades ago. It was not difficult to see that each of them felt frustrations from the other's beliefs and mutual judgments. My uncle did not see an entrepreneurial partner in my father, and the latter was very trustworthy and hardworking and did not feel acknowledged enough by my uncle. Certainly neither was aware of the limitations each of them might have brought into the business relationship concerning managerial, production, marketing, and relational issues.

In spite of the incredibly harsh circumstances of my mother's life, she apparently did a good job raising her children. The four of us are professionals, decent people, and have led reasonable lives. Nevertheless I have to admit that living with her was difficult. There was no space for having fun "just because" or for real celebration. She did like to host dinners during which she never sat and worked all the time while the guests were at the table. She returned a slight smile when receiving congratulations for a beautifully laid-out table or a delicious meal. Mother was capricious, unpredictable, and had frequent nervous breakdowns for no reason. My father insisted that we should not anger her and do whatever she wanted, since those were the instructions given by a psychiatrist whom they had visited. But sometimes it was difficult to know what exactly she wanted. If she became annoyed with one of us, she would wait for my father to arrive home from work and start shouting and complaining nonstop about the horrible child who did not want to put on this or that sweater. My father became nervous and hit us. Actually my elder brother and I were more rebellious than the others (meaning we said out loud what we thought), and received more beatings than the younger ones. By the way, I always considered my twin brother to be younger than I.

Secrets were the norm at our home, so that whatever information we wanted to know about our family was received only through my cousin's nanny, or I should say my elder brother's cousin's nanny. I remember how shocked I was when I discovered that this brother was not the son of our mother. This might have meant that he was not really our blood brother. I was about six years old and had asked my mother why my brother's second last name was different from that of the rest of the siblings.[4]

"You will know when you'll be older," was the answer this time, the same response as it always was whenever we asked her something that was complicated for her to think about or reply to. "Why later?" I insisted. "Because such is life," she replied, and that was the end of the conversation until the next time a question arose and I would receive a similar answer.

My elder brother suspected the truth but he was not sure. We all went to ask his cousin's nanny if she knew the answer. There we were, three boys and a girl (my little sister was too small), pushing the woman to tell us the truth. Finally she did so. I still remember how my heart beat fast and I remained speechless during the long minutes it took for her to recount the story. I was definitely not in the habit of being speechless while at home. In fact my parents had already declared that I would probably be a lawyer because I was usually asking

---

4. In Chile we use our first and second given names plus our father's surname, and then our mother's surname. Married women do not legally change their surnames.

questions, demanding to know the answers, and arguing again and again when there were no answers or when they did not satisfy me. In the end I became an engineer and not a lawyer. It was very important to me to compete with my two brothers, who are also engineers, and show the world that we, women, are as intelligent and able as men are.

Growing up I realized that my father had overprotected my mother so much that he did not allow her to overcome her trauma, despite his best intentions. Never in her life did she have the opportunity to define and design who she really wanted to be. My father would not even agree to teach her how to write a check. I think she must have been a very smart woman and could have managed her own business, but her impotent past and my father's overprotection did their job in eroding her self-confidence. She never had the opportunity to develop self-esteem and self-confidence, and my siblings and I think that she imposed that way of being on us. I will even go further and claim that she suffered from "survival syndrome," which made her feel guilty for having survived the war while losing her mother, family, and friends. She was not prepared to let us, her children, be whole beings. I think she was not given the time and the psychological space to heal from her trauma.

There came a time when the four of us needed to leave her. My elder brother and I got married, respectively, within three weeks of each other, and the other two left the country a year later. My twin brother was twenty-two and my sister was eighteen when they left their birthplace, never again to go back to live in Chile. Both my elder brother and I had children, got divorced, and much later found our present partners.

When I was a young girl, my mother delegated certain motherly functions to me. For instance, she could not bring herself to tell my eight-year-old sister about menstruation. She was worried that her periods could start ahead of time because of certain symptoms, so she asked me to tell her. While writing this now, I realize that I do not remember how I, myself, learned about it. Presumably it was not through my mother. When she became older, and was already a widow, she once told me that everyone had a mother except for her and she needed one badly, so she asked me to play that role. I felt very awkward when I heard her request, and I must admit that I also felt that I had never had a loving, protecting mother myself. Yet I instantly realized that I had actually been playing that role since my father had passed away. That day I promised her that I would listen to and take care of her, and she thanked me with the voice of a little girl. From then on I deliberately behaved like a mother towards her.

Another important trait of my mother is that she had the habit of threatening whomever she was angry with to take her own life. Nobody took this threat too seriously until one day she took many times more than the prescribed amount of her sleeping pills, and it was extremely difficult to wake her up. I must have been about eight years old. I remember feeling angry and not sad. Later on it seemed to me that this was her way of punishing herself and the world for the demons and ghosts that tortured her. I remember two more of these suicidal attempts while I was young. In the latter, I was seventeen and alone with her at the beach. She had been complaining that my father was inconsiderate by inventing faraway trips he needed to take during the summer when the family was supposed to take their vacations together at the seaside house. It was the beginning of our summer holidays and my siblings were not there. I sensed that she was jealous of someone, but she never explained her feelings. She just went into her bedroom and took many pills. When I saw that she would not wake up, I left her alone while I fetched a friend of hers who was staying at the same beach, and between the two of us we woke her up with difficulty.

My mother must have had many hidden values. She had incredibly good and faithful friends, and she brought up educated and well-prepared children to face their own lives with strength and dignity. She passed away in 2006, and I remember her with great love, tenderness, and admiration for all she was able to overcome with such few tools: intuition, modesty, hidden intelligence, and also, I guess, a certain degree of manipulation.

Now It's Your Turn[5]

One of the most important things I have learned since becoming a gestalt therapist and a coach is the value of a deep, good question. Take a brief moment to ask yourself the following:

---

5. This book is an invitation to think, ask many questions, and reflect. If you want to ask me a question, make a comment, or let me know your answers to my questions, please contact me at www.thenovelentrepreneur.com.

- Do you usually ask questions?
- What kinds of questions are they?
- Do you think you have learned from them? What?
- Do you ask questions about yourself?
- Have you discovered something about you after asking those questions?

You might have noticed that in the last section I gave you some hints about my early years. It is not my entire biography. The story I told reflects answers that I have received in the course of my life and elaborated on. I still have some unanswered questions about myself, the people closest to me during my early years, and the decisions I made or did not make during my lifetime.

Both the questions and the answers might be influenced by my interpretations, or in other words, the story I have told myself about my early years; specifically by the challenges I have overcome and the ones I have not, by instances of awareness I might have experienced, and by all kinds of feelings and emotions. My interpretations are the stories I tell myself that make sense to me.

If there is one thing that will help you live a fruitful and fulfilled life, it is the awareness of who you are; where you come from; who are the people you think have been responsible for determining how your life was and is, including the role you yourself have played; and what challenges you have had to face or are facing right now. Awareness is a condition that is necessary to reach fulfillment. It is my belief that we need to experience over and over the relationship between awareness and fulfillment. That is why I invite you several times to practice it in the course of this book. I now invite you to do the following exercise:

> Write the story of your early years, and make a list of questions such as:
> - In **what way** and **who** conditioned you to feel or do **what**?
> - Are you a victim of your circumstances, or do you think you are responsible for determining how your life is now and how it will be in the future?
> - Write down as many questions as you possibly can.
> - Read again the section "My Early Years," and see what new questions about your life come up.

The will to do this exercise, the attention you give to everything that you experience during this process, and the discipline to go all the way and finish the exercise will tell you how accurate your awareness of yourself is and can be, and also how prepared you are to embark on the journey towards your fulfillment. **Will, Attention, Discipline**. I call these the "Three Graces." They will be our faithful companions, both in your reading and in my writing of this book. They are divine gifts that life provides you for your journey towards fulfillment.

CHAPTER 2

Facts and Interpretations

Suppose you see a middle-aged woman stepping up onto the sidewalk from the street. Your eyes look at her legs, which show torn stockings. From where you are, you do not see blood on her knees. You keep watching until she stands straight, draws her hands to her hips, then moves them to her back, just below her waist. She starts walking slowly, with an arm supported by another woman. After a while they separate and each continues on their own way.

When you reach home, you tell what you saw to your son, daughter, or spouse.

- Imagine what your posture and your tone of voice would be.
- Pay attention to your breathing and assess if it is your normal rhythm, or faster, or slower.
- Check how you feel at this moment, and what words you would use to describe your feelings.
- Write down your feelings and words.

Keep in mind that there is no right or wrong way to tell this story. Now that there are two versions of it, yours and mine:

- Did we both, you and I, tell the same story?
- Did we do it in a similar way?
- Did we use more or less the same words?

If you read my account of the story again, you will notice that I tell what I saw, as if I were a camera filming the scene. I did not contribute any of my feelings, thoughts, or interpretations in this narration. I only accounted for facts that I observed outside of myself. This is not the way in which we usually tell a story or relate an incident that we experience to another person. We usually put more of ourselves in the stories we tell. You might have thought that she fell, or that someone had pushed her, and that is why her stockings were torn. You could have made that assumption as soon as you saw her, yet you became paralyzed and helpless, even though you might have wanted to run and help the woman.

FACTS AND INTERPRETATIONS

- What else would you have told your son, daughter, or spouse?
- How would you have felt?

I observed and narrated facts. I did not give any interpretation or explanation regarding the facts I displayed. Nevertheless, what we normally do is not that. We normally mix facts with our interpretation of them. This is what I did in the section "My Early Years" in the previous chapter. We, human beings, are creative creatures because our brains and our language allow us to be so. In that sense, we are all alike. That is why we can interpret and explain what we see beyond recalling the simple existing facts. We can create stories that seem valid to us when interpreting facts. What I described as my early years in the previous chapter is not a universal truth; it is only my story. Perhaps my siblings' stories are different. My guess is that not only are some of the interpretations different and, nevertheless, valid, but that they also might choose different facts to tell their own stories.

I am inviting you to look in depth at the distinction between a fact, which we observe in the world, (the **What**) and our interpretations and assumptions, which allow us to find explanations that make sense to us (the **How**, the **Why**, and the **What For**). When we express facts, we are merely describing what we observe in the outside world. A fact is not perceived within your particular way of being. In this book I shall call your particular way of being your *soul*. Again, facts are there in the world, not in your soul. You find the facts in the realm of a community that gives the same name to each fact.

An interpretation, in turn, is the work of your unique self. It belongs to you. It can certainly be shared and accepted, thus becoming a part of other people's selves. For example, scientific explanations are accepted as valid (notice that valid is not the same as true) if a certain commonly accepted method of interpretation by the scientific community is used to formulate an explanation.

In order to interpret, you need to first observe the facts. You can trust observations made by yourself or others, such as authors, scientists, professors, or just someone you know, if you can find evidence for the observations described by them. This is enough to ascertain that the facts are true. If, and only if, the facts are true, you can proceed to interpret and find explanations. Interpretations are never true. They are valid if they are supported by true facts, or invalid if they are not.

To summarize, facts belong to the outside world that we observe, and they can be true or false. Interpretations can be considered a form of putting these facts together and organizing and elaborating them in order to make sense of the world in which we live. We are unique in terms of what sense we make of this world. Not all that makes sense to me will make sense to you. Coming back to the scene of the woman in the street, you and I both observed facts. We did not necessarily perceive the same facts and did not make sense of them in the same way, since your interpretation of what is relevant to look at, and of what you saw, might be different from my interpretation and from what I saw.

First we observe facts, and then we build interpretations that allow us to explain and make sense of them. Each person can have a different interpretation of the same fact or set of facts that everyone observed, or you yourself might find more than one valid interpretation of them. I cannot help remembering an old song that I love. It is Paul Simon's song, "50 Ways to Leave Your Lover." I am humming it right now, as I write these words.

There are many ways in which we can make sense of our observations, and we have the capacity to choose the ones we consider the best for us and for the systems to which we belong. By the way, it can be fun to come up with two or three different interpretations about the story of the woman in the street.

An interpretation can be compared to a work of art. If it conveys sense and meaning, it will be considered a good interpretation, just like the quality of the writer's narrative, the painter's work, or the musician's playing. An interpretation is richer depending on the number of facts it considers. The richer the interpretation, the easier it is to create a story that makes sense.

Now think about your daily life. Does the following describe the way you operate in daily life? You gather the facts, organize them, tell yourself a certain number of different stories about those facts, and finally choose the one you feel and think is the best for your life and those of the people around you.

- Is this what you usually do?

I invite you to stop for a while, bring together your present feelings and thoughts, and read again the former paragraph, several times. See if something changes in your body, feelings, or thoughts.

Then ask yourself:
- Is this what I really do?
- Do I separate fact from interpretation?
- Would I like to try a different way of interpreting the challenges of my life?
- How do I feel right now?

I sincerely expect you to be a little confused. If that is the case, the reason for this is that we usually do not separate these distinctions. Furthermore, it is very common to operate the other way around in daily life. We usually interpret first and then consider our interpretation as a fact.

Let me give you an example in the following dialogue between two friends, Maya and Lisa.

L: "You know, Maya, I'm never going to talk to Eric again. This is it!"
M: "But Lisa, you sound so angry. What happened?"
L: "I bet you would have been furious if he would have done it to you."

FACTS AND INTERPRETATIONS

M: "What are you talking about, Lisa?"

L: "Well, we were supposed to meet at Starbucks to plan the project, you know, and he simply forgot and kept me waiting. I lost an hour of my life!"

M: "Oh, that's awful, Lisa. I'm sorry for you. Are you sure he forgot?"

L: "Of course, I'm sure, Maya! What else could have happened? If he knew he was going to be late he could have called me instead of kept me waiting."

M: "Yeah, that's true. Anyway, Lisa, if I bump into him may I ask him what happened?"

L: "That's up to you, Maya, but don't come to me with the issue. I don't want to hear a single excuse, and he is already out of my life. I am looking for another partner to work together on the project."

M: "Okay. I'll do my best to help you, Lisa. Bye for now."

I have some questions for you:
- Have you ever been in a similar situation? If you have, write it down.
- In the dialogue above, which are facts and which are interpretations?
- Distinguish facts and interpretations in the story you just wrote down.
- Is somebody having a bad time in the dialogue above? If yes, do you know the reason?

- Remember if somebody was uneasy in the story you wrote and what might have caused the bad feelings.
- Do Maya and Lisa feel the same? Do they share the same attitude towards the incident? If the answer is no to either question, what is the difference in feelings and/or attitudes?
- Would Lisa have been as angry as she was if Eric had called her earlier to tell her that he would be very late or would not be able to meet her?

My interpretation of the situation is that Lisa considers it a fact that Eric forgot his appointment with her. Nevertheless, nobody has told Lisa what made Eric fail to meet her. So the only known fact is that Eric did not show up at Starbucks when he was supposed to, according to Lisa's knowledge.

Now I invite you to:
- Make as many interpretations as you can about this situation.
- Gather (invent) more facts in order to enrich your interpretation.

I'll start the discussion. What if Lisa and Eric wrote down a different place, a different day, or a different time to meet in their schedules? Knowing these are facts and not interpretations, we can know them just by asking the parties involved in this scenario.

FACTS AND INTERPRETATIONS

Confusing facts with interpretations leads to one of the most prevalent misunderstandings in human communication. It disconnects people and makes them suffer. That is why I am asking you to pay attention to this distinction. Understanding the difference between them and using them correctly in language is a gateway for creativity (interpretation) and lack of suffering. (Facts are facts, and we all observe them as such. We do not need to guess.) The distinction between fact and interpretation is like shadows or echoes accompanying you throughout this book together with the Three Graces: **Will, Attention, and Discipline.**

"Get your facts first, and then you can distort them as much as you please."[6]

---

6. Rudyard Kipling, "An Interview with Mark Twain," p. 180, *From Sea to Sea: Letters of Travel*, Doubleday & McClure Company, 1899

CHAPTER 3

Is Your Glass Half Empty or Half Full?

You might have heard the following story. If so, please read it remembering my invitation to be curious and to look at things with an open heart and from different angles. Here is the story:

Two shoe salesmen were sent to Africa to see if there was a market for their product.

The first salesman reported back, "There is no business opportunity here. No one wears shoes."

The second salesman reported back, "This is a fantastic business opportunity! No one wears shoes."

- What would your report have been if you were one of the shoe salesmen?
- Is your glass half empty or half full?

Whatever answer you give will be good, as it will be yours. You might like it or not. If you like it, I understand you are content with the life you are living and you realize that there is always room for improvement. If you do not like it, you probably desire to improve or make changes in your life. Whatever your answer, I invite you to do an inner journey of exploration. You will need to take some tools and instruments so as to build an appropriate road map that will allow you to discover what you are looking for in the first place.

This book is intended to provide you with a toolkit for discovering where you want to go, designing your path, creating the necessary environment for building it, and starting your journey.

- What are you going to look for? Take some time to ask the question and write down some possible answers.
- How do you see your glass? Is it half full or half empty?

In the previous chapter I defined your soul as your particular way of being, as that which distinguishes you from any other human being. We shall go one step further now and distinguish your soul from your personality. Your soul is not affected by the circumstances that condition your behavior. It is the point of connection with the elements of the universe, including living beings. Does it happen to you that when you say or hear the word *soul* you relate it to something spiritual? That's what it does to me.

Contrary to your soul, you develop your unique personality by including the environmental conditions that surround you during your upbringing, and also your temperament, which is derived from genetic and other biological factors. Your behavior is largely an expression of your personality. This means that you are not completely autonomous to choose whether to see the glass as half full or half empty, since your biological make-up, your lineage, and the environment that surrounds you affect your choices, making them unconscious ones.

Suppose you are conducting a survey with one question: Is the glass half full or half empty? Considering a reasonable sample—let's say you poll at least two thousand people—what would the result of the survey be?

My hypothesis is that 60% or more of the people will answer "half empty." This forecast is based on the fact that there are hundreds of studies indicating that the perception of bad is stronger than the perception of good.[7] Bad events produce more impact than good ones, and therefore they are more powerful in every field of life, such as everyday events, close relationships, social network patterns, interpersonal interactions, and learning processes. Our perceptions of bad emotions, bad parents, and bad feedback are stronger than the good ones. Bad impressions and bad stereotypes are quicker to form and more resistant to change than good ones.

---

7. R. F. Baumeister et al., "Bad is Stronger than Good," *Review of General Psychology* 2001, vol.5 pp.323-370.

Here are some examples: While a good day has no lasting effect on the following day, a bad day carries over. We process negative data faster and more thoroughly than positive data, and that affects us longer. Socially, we invest more in avoiding a bad reputation than in building a good one. Emotionally, we go to greater lengths to avoid a bad mood than to experience a good one. Pessimists tend to assess their health more accurately than optimists. People—even babies as young as six months old—are quick to spot an angry face in a crowd, but slower to pick out a happy one. In fact, no matter how many smiles you see in that crowd, you will always spot the angry face first.[8] In short, we are good at feeling pain, but less so at feeling the absence of it.

Let us suppose you belong to the potential majority of people who tend to see the glass as half empty. What would the world look like for you? I invite you to write down all the calamities and threats that the world is experiencing now.

I have listed some of my worries, which I call:

Bad Things That Are Happening in the World

- Worldwide terrorism
- Unstable world economy
- Global warming
- Nuclear threat
- Religious fanaticism coupled with warfare technology

---

8. J. Burak, "Humans Are Hardwired for Negativity," *AEON Magazine*, September 6, 2014.

- Scarcity of natural resources such as water, energy, and useful soil
- Massive migrations
- Poverty
- Urban delinquency
- General uncertainty

Are my worries your worries? If that is the case, you might be wondering why I am writing this book. I invited you to learn how to create a path for fulfillment and make the journey, and now I am saying that most of us are much more inclined to negativity than to a positive response to the challenges that our systems and the environment present us. And the challenges are huge.

Is there anything good going on in the world? Yes, there is,[9] and I call it:

Good Things That Are Happening in the World[10]

- World peace. The general tendency between 1940 and 2012 is a strong decrease in casualties due to war and terrorism: between 2000 and 2012 they are 50% less than between 1990 and 2000; 75% less than between 1960 and 1990, and 99% less than between 1940 and 1950.
- **Economic stability.** The forecast of growth for this decade (2010-2020) is 10 to 20% higher than during the previous

---
9. F. Zakaria, Commencement Speech, Harvard University, May 2012. https://www.youtube.com/watch?v=aAj5oevN93k
10. S. Pinker, *The Better Angels of our Nature,* Viking Press, 2011.

decade, 60% higher than two decades ago, and five times higher than three decades ago.
- **Poverty reduction.** In the last fifty years, poverty has decreased more than in the last five hundred years, mostly during the last twenty years.
- **Increase in life expectancy.** One of each three children born in 2012 and beyond in the developed world will live more than one hundred years.
- **Scientific and technological development.** Exponential growth in computing capacity, connectivity, neuroscience, genetics, and material sciences. All this can bring more effective warfare to light but also better means for enormous health improvement and well-being in the world. Science and technology are not good or bad as such. It is their application by human beings that grant them a moral value. The same science and technological principles that are used to develop modern weaponry are also used for medical purposes that will increase the world's health and longevity.
- **Significant world increase in the amount of higher education graduates.** In the last forty years, male graduates have increased four times, and female graduates have increased seven times.

Did you notice that I wrote facts that can validate the "good things" while I did not validate with facts the "bad things"? Why do you think I did that?

IS YOUR GLASS HALF EMPTY OR HALF FULL?

This chapter started with some bad news. Please ask yourself now, as honestly as you possibly can: Would you have seen the good news about the same issues (war and terrorism casualties, poverty, and economic stability) with the same open eyes as you saw the bad news; or would you really have needed the given data to validate the very good news? Is your glass half full or half empty?

In 1982, Princeton University psychologist Dr. Daniel Kahneman coined the term *loss aversion* to describe his finding that we mourn loss more than we enjoy benefit. The upset felt after losing a thousand dollars is always greater than the happiness felt after gaining the same amount.[11]

- Close your eyes and ask yourself: Does this happen to me?

In terms of interactions, University of Washington psychologist John Gottman found a formula in 1992 to predict divorce with an accuracy rate of more than 90% by spending only fifteen minutes with a newlywed couple.[12] He spent the time evaluating the ratio of positive to negative expressions exchanged between the partners, including gestures and body language. Gottman reported that couples needed a "magic ratio" of at least five positive expressions for each negative one

---

11. Kahneman et al, eds. *Judgement under Uncertainty: Heuristics and Biases*, Cambridge University Press, 1982. Kahneman was awarded The Nobel Prize in Economics in 2002, despite his being a psychologist, for his theory on decision-making under uncertainty.
12. J. Gottman and Nan Silver, *The Seven Principles for Making Marriage Work*, Crown Publishers, 1999.

if a relationship was to survive. I suggest you exercise this ratio with your significant other.

- Learn what ratio of positive to negative comments you and your partner have now.
- See if you can raise your ratio to at least 5:1. Can you?
- Can your partner do the same?

Couples who divorced had an average of four negative comments to three positive ones.

In the corporate world, the Chilean psychologist Marcial Losada[13] studied sixty management teams at a large information-processing company. In the most effective groups, employees were praised at a ratio of six times for their good work versus every single time they were put down. There were almost three negative remarks to every positive one in especially low-performing groups. It seems to me that by retaining the ratio of 5:1 in any domain of your life you can do reasonably well as a member of a team or as a spouse, parent, or friend.

Many authors suggest that the perception "bad is stronger than good" must have been a necessary Darwinian adaptive trait of the early stages of the human species when people had to move around to make a living. Men hunted and women gathered crops while carrying their children around. All sorts of dangers from nature threatened them, so it must have been crucial to be able to discern the negative possibilities very

---

13. M. Losada and other, "The Role of Positivity and Connectivity in the Performance of Business Teams: A Nonlinear Dynamics Model," *American Behavioral Scientist* 2004 vol. 47 no. 6, February 2004.

quickly. Survival requires urgent attention to possible bad outcomes, but less urgent attention to good ones.

We shall later examine neuroscientific findings of the last twenty years that are considered revolutionary and are changing the way we look at our neurobiology and its relationship to our behavior and social interaction. Many of these findings are readily applicable in the fields of medicine, pharmacology, psychiatry, psychology, and coaching, since today we can count on scientific data that correlates very well with many of our philosophical assumptions and professional practices. These findings validate that bad is perceptually stronger than good.

But, on the other hand, neuroscience is making daily discoveries about how our brains work that will inevitably lead us to use more of our brains and certainly better than we do now. You will see that if you learn to be aware—that is, if you are able to understand who you are and how you relate to the world, what you really enjoy and dislike, and your values and beliefs; if you know what your temperament is and how your actions affect other people, how you have developed your personality, what conditionings and challenges you have worked out, and what challenges you still have to overcome—it will not be difficult for you to know what you need to learn in order to make the journey on a path that will lead you to a fulfilling life.

We shall follow step by step the development of this awareness when using my method PEL-MET (Presence, Emotions, and Language Method). You can start exploring now how you learn best and what your talents and abilities are, and also what your distinctive personality traits, worldview, and values are. Fulfillment requires you to know all this about yourself.

I related to awareness before and will continue doing so throughout the book. Why? Because pursuing awareness of yourself is a precondition for the journey I am inviting you to take with me. If you find some repetitions, do not worry. I will purposely repeat some comments, questions, and distinctions because **repetition** is an essential action for obtaining desired learning. Learning manifests itself in practice and in behavior. It is by no means an accumulation of information in some part of the brain. And I want you and me to learn how to become self-aware and acquire dexterity in the use of the Three Graces: **Will, Attention, and Discipline.** These are three gifts the universe offers that are everywhere, and we are free to use them whenever we feel the need to do so. When we combine these gifts with repetition, there is learning. You will have transformed yourself in the areas in which learning took place. You will also create new automatic behaviors, which we shall call **new habits.**

Here are some more questions for you:
- How do you learn?
- Do you visualize a role for repetition? What? Where?

Seeing the glass as half full is what optimists do. If you are not one by temperament, you can learn to see the glass in this way. Research has shown that people who see the glass as half full are not only happier, but also wealthier and healthier.

IS YOUR GLASS HALF EMPTY OR HALF FULL?

You might be interested in asking yourself some questions and doing some exercises that take you out of your comfort zone, but in the long run lead you to fulfillment.

I will ask the first question: When you analyze yourself or a project you are developing, do you concentrate on your strengths or on your weaknesses? The answer to this question allows you to predict whether your world is half full or half empty.

CHAPTER 4

How You See Yourself: Strengths and Weaknesses

A great deal of your life is spent making decisions. I do not mean that you are constantly making decisions that will alter your life; in fact, you make many of them unconsciously without asking yourself any questions at all. When you drive your car, you stop at the red lights and accelerate at the green lights without making a decision. It is already incorporated in your brain and expressed as a habit.

But suppose you don't feel well, and you have been in bed the whole day. Do you get out of bed automatically to brush your teeth before going to sleep, or do you ask yourself if you have enough energy to get up and do something that is part of the routine of your life? I confess I have asked this explicit question more than once, and the answer has not always been the one indicated by my routine. More than once I have stayed in bed without brushing my teeth, altering my habitual way of doing things.

Our lives are full of routines. If that were not so, I don't think we could live. We would not have the time. Routines determine behaviors that turn into habits. Just like any other animal, we are creatures of habit, and sometimes we must make conscious decisions. Notice that before deciding to brush my teeth, even though I was feeling ill and had no energy, I asked myself the question whether to do it or not.

After decision, what usually comes next is action. If you are involved in the actions that you will take as a consequence of your decision, you will probably think about yourself. If that is the case, where do you start? Do you ask yourself what you can do in order to make the right decision? Or do you wonder, "Am I good enough or will I probably fall or fail?" In other words, do you start by asking what's good about you or what's bad about you? Is the glass half full or half empty? This is no different from putting your psychological weight on your strengths or on your weaknesses.

Considering what you read above about our natural tendency to highlight the negative and not the positive facts of life, I expect it is easier for you to start reflecting about your weaknesses than about your strengths. When it comes to the latter, you might even feel reluctant to ask yourself what they are. If you are a woman, you might have internalized that being modest is virtuous. Many of my female clients have discovered that the modesty they were taught to revere was really a mandate to appear virtuously invisible. Do you notice the paradox?

Actually, all of us have been taught by traditional psychology, which is rooted in medical science, to see ourselves with the eyes of illness; that when something is wrong with us we need to be cured.

I challenge you to start asking questions in areas of action that are far from automatic for you. Let's try answering the following question: "Should I stay in my current job or should I look for something that will bring more fun into my life?" I invite you to stop reading, and do the following exercise:

> Read the following question out loud:
> "Should I keep my job, or should I look for something that will bring more fun into my life?"
> - Let the answer come naturally to you.
> - What is the answer?
> - How did you feel when answering this question?

Let's play a little more with this exercise. Did you start thinking about your weaknesses, stop there, decide that you are bored but you are paying the price to have a comfortable life, and decide to stay where you are? Or did you feel confused, with mixed emotions, and decide to postpone the decision?

Perhaps you started by asking yourself, "Is the change really going to bring greater fun and joy into my life?" (I like that question.) If this happened, what would happen next?

We all have strengths and we all have weaknesses. In this book we shall consider strengths as talents and qualities that you have or that come easily to you and that you like to use or to engage in. You can identify strengths by tying talents to delight. We need both in our lives. It is not enough to be good at playing the piano while hating the kind of life a pianist leads.

A Gallup poll found that 70% of Americans hate their businesses or jobs, or have completely "checked out" from them, while they let time go and feel less fulfilled day by day.[14] People have skills and use them, but that is not enough to have a satisfying job. Let's not confuse skills with strengths.

Can you imagine how much both productivity and well-being could rise if only we asked ourselves what our talents are and how we can match them with a joyful way of using them? Do you think you could live a better life?

It is interesting to observe that the science of psychology has been moving in the direction of health instead of illness to study individuals' behavior. In 1998, Professor Martin Seligman took advantage of his position as president of the American Association of Psychologists to launch a new branch in the science of psychology. He gave it the name "Positive Psychology" in honor of Abraham Maslow,[15] who was the first

---

14. Gallup's "State of the American Workplace" report. The report highlights findings from Gallup's study of the American workplace from 2010 through 2012.
15. Abraham Maslow, psychologist best known for his development of the widely used Hierarchy of Needs.

psychologist to use the term. While explaining his theory of well-being and separating Positive Psychology from other more traditional branches of psychology, Seligman said:

> "The goal of understanding well-being and of generating conditions for a life that can make it possible is not, in any case, identical to the goal of understanding misery and dissolving the conditions of life that do not enable it."[16]

Seligman has proposed twenty-four strengths, which he calls **Character Strengths**. They are not related to specific skills you might have. He developed a questionnaire that allows you to determine your character strengths.[17] From that point on, it will be easier to find out which of your skills need your strengths. You might want to develop new character strengths and widen the scope of your own world. I am not saying that struggling against a tendency that might come from our own biology or conditioning (a weakness) will be an easy task, but it is necessary to remember that learning and awareness are also related to our biology. This is what makes me think that we can change the tendency towards the bad. There will come a time when the natural tendency of human beings will be to discover how to combine strengths (understood as the combination of talent, skill, and thrill), Seligman's character strengths, and fun and joy while progressively expanding the horizons of what is possible in this world as a whole and in the world of each person on the planet. In other words, we can

---

16. M. Seligman, *Flourish*, Free Press, 2012.
17. http://www.viacharacter.org/www/Character-Strengths/VIA-Classification

discover and use the gifts that are there for us to take, and then improve the lives of everyone.

Would you like that? If your answer is yes, you can gather the tools you have been given so far and start working right now. My suggestion is to:

- List your talents.
- Grade the joy of using each talent.
- List your talents according to the joy grade. (The first one is your best.)
- List your strengths. Include talents from the previous list that you feel provide enough joy to qualify as strengths.
- Go to Seligman's questionnaire and discover your character strengths and virtues.
- Take each of your strengths and ask yourself if you are using it at its full capacity in several domains of your life, and particularly in your job.

If you work on this exercise, you will find an excellent tool to bring into your life. Here it is, ready for you to use right away.

The time has come to make your decisions and act according to your strengths. It is not necessary to overcome all your weaknesses in order to enjoy your work and live a good life. You can overcome only those weaknesses that block you from being who you want to be or doing what you want to do. The way to do this is through learning. Repeat this exercise, or ask for help until you are able to find your strengths and use them repeatedly in the best possible ways until you don't need additional help. When you become aware of your strengths and learn to use them, your life will become joyous, fertile, fruitful, connected, loving, and fulfilled.

CHAPTER 5

The Observers That You Are

Are You One and Only?

You have already seen that we, human beings, are all alike as a species; similar yet different from others in our biological make-up, culture, beliefs, and professions; and unique in our souls, that is, our particular way of being, which belongs to us and to nobody else. Our souls connect us to the universe, to the mystery of life, to that which we sense and feel and cannot put into words.

It is my understanding that in your particular way of being you will not find a "real" you as a homogenous, fixed, and solid observer. Rather, your "you" is composed of a number of different observers who look at things from different angles, allowing you to see and perceive different things, set different goals, and sustain different beliefs within yourself. Do you ever feel unsure about what it is you really want? Or have you wanted something badly and an entity within you, like a hidden evil demon, sabotages you and doesn't allow you to get what you want? You might even hear a voice within you saying something like "Who do you think you are?" People call these voices "hidden beliefs," "the unconscious mind," or "shadows." You can consider these situations as power struggles between two or more observers within you who want to lead you to different places and want you to be a different person and do different things.

In order to have a fulfilled life, you will need to have a strong will and acute attention, and explore in a disciplined way the observers in you who are blocking the path towards defining and pursuing your purpose in life, work, parenthood, or whatever field is important to you. (Note the presence of what were defined previously as the Three Graces.

Context and Observers

Not only do you have several observers with contradictory desires, depending on the standpoint of each observer, you are able to "see" only a part of the global environment that surrounds you. Suppose you are sitting at a table having dinner with your family. What you see with your eyes is different from what everybody else sees. You can see what others cannot, and others can see what you cannot. The physical reality that can be seen by every person is different.

Your environment is not fixed and unique. Your observations will not be the same if the context or the environment in which you observe changes. Here is an example of what I mean:

A few years ago, while visiting family in California, I bought a camera. The day I arrived back in Santiago, in late winter, August, it had rained the day before, and the sky was clear, intensely blue. The Andes Mountains were covered with very white snow and there was no smog, which is rare at that time of the year in Santiago. It was a perfect occasion to try my camera, so I took a picture of the spectacular view.

Days later, there were beautiful clouds creating a strange, luminous effect from their contact with a faltering sun. I took another picture from the same spot as before. What do you think happened? The picture was beautiful, but there was no way to guess that it was the same landscape as the first one, although the photo had been taken from exactly the same spot.

Since then I have taken hundreds of photos at different times of day and season from the same spot. All of them are different. When I took each photo, I did not observe the same reality even though I always stood at the same spot. The environment is continually changing, so not only do different observers see differently, but one single observer does not always see the same view.

Different people have different observers who can see and perceive differently. The distance from which you observe can also change what you see. You can find a great example of this in the portraits of the painter Victor Molev.[18]

- Visit his website.
- Look at his portraits.
- When you recognize the person represented in the portrait, click on it.
- Let me know your observations at www.thenovelentrepreneur.com

There are things you simply cannot observe. Suppose you have a feather on your head, which fell from a passing bird. You did not see it falling or feel it landing on you. Can you observe yourself walking around with a feather on your head?

What can you say about reality when you consider the potential multitude of observers in varying contexts?

The Observer Who Observes the Observer

The observer is not only some part of you that sees the outside world. The observer also has the capacity to look at your inner self, and that capacity has nothing to do with the sensory organ of the eye. Rather, what this observer sees, from a certain point of view, is a combination of your body (your physical presence and your biological nature), and your feelings and thoughts, which are accessible from that viewpoint. As

---

18. V. Molev: http://www.victormolev.com/portrait/portrait1.htm

THE OBSERVERS THAT YOU ARE

you saw above, you can have some encouraging observers coexisting with others who are disheartening, depending on the point of view and the context surrounding the observer. Likewise, some of them can be flexible and others rigid. These polarities can create diverse power struggles within you. For instance, if the observer represents social conditioning, and the mandate received by a girl at an early age was "You must not be very visible," this observer will rigidly concentrate on the invisibility of this person; whereas, if the observer who is looking and listening desires for her to think big and reach a better place, that observer will probably be more flexible and will try to push her out of her comfort and conditioned zone into a learning space. The rigid observers and the flexible observers compete with each other, each one trying to lead the person towards their particular perspectives and viewpoints.

It is possible to think of a different entity, capable of distinguishing the different observers who push or pull you in different directions. Let's call it the "observer of the observers." The mission of this new type of observer is solely to watch and register without making any judgment. This observer simply looks, sees, and registers what they observe.

The following metaphor might help you better understand the notion of the observer of the observers, and also what its purpose in your life is. Imagine a three-story building in which the first and second floors have glass ceilings and the third floor has no ceiling or roof at all. The first floor has several rooms. Each one is different and is populated by one or more observers engaged in different activities and interacting in different ways. Along comes the observer of the observers who climbs the stairs to the second floor. That floor has only one room. He (or she) positions himself in such a way that he can observe all of what is going on on the first floor. He does so, writing down everything he observes. They are only facts, and he does not have the capacity to judge. But he does have a panoramic view of all that is going on on the first floor simultaneously. The observers on the first floor do not have this capacity since there are walls separating the rooms, and besides, they are completely engaged in their actions and interactions.

After writing down what he saw, the observer of the observers climbs to the third floor, where he meets another observer. This new observer is your soul. Soul has already been defined in this book as your particular way of being, which is not affected by the circumstances that condition your behavior. Your soul is your point of connection to the elements of the universe, including living beings. Your soul is on the third floor, with no ceiling or roof over it. It connects you to the universe and gives you the gifts you need according to the facts presented by the observer of the observers, and, at the same time, it returns what you no longer need back to the universe.

Did you notice that judgment could happen only on the first floor? You can choose to let go of your fear, climb the stairs to the second floor, observe your observers, and then reach your soul. These are territories in which there is no judging and no fear. Knowing this gives you more freedom and more

THE OBSERVERS THAT YOU ARE

power to choose, and also offers the possibility to reduce the gap between where you are and where you want to be.

The observer of the observers is a powerful tool for self-exploration leading to more knowledge about your inner self. I invite you to use it!

When I was trained in gestalt therapy, I was taught an exercise that has become very powerful in many of my coaching sessions. It is called "The Empty Chair." I use it whenever my client and I discover two conflicting observers who are not allowing my client to freely walk the steps towards achieving their purpose.

Let's imagine you are my client and we discover there is tension between your ambition to accept a leading position that was offered to you at your workplace and something that pulls you down and diminishes your wish to take the step. You find yourself saying, "No, I will have less time for my family. I have never been in charge of other people, and it will be terrible. I don't want to quarrel. I want to be liked by everyone. I'm not born for something like this. I don't want to manage people. I don't know how to do it."

The first step is to turn these two observers into characters such as those in a play, who are described very specifically and will determine a certain way of being and behaving. You can give each character a name, or name them **A** and **B**, whatever makes you feel more comfortable. Notice that now there are four characters in the room: **you, me, A,** and **B**. After specifying the attributes of **A** and **B**, you will play both of them, and **you** will not participate in the conversation that follows.

The second step is to place two chairs facing each other. **A** will sit on one chair, and **B** will sit on the other, alternately, so that there is always an empty chair.

You decide who starts the conversation. **Me** has the role of listening and giving orientation if needed. For example:

A will be the observer who wants to get the job.
B will be the observer who pulls **you** down.
B starts the conversation:

B: "How can you even consider accepting this promotion?! Don't you know how it will affect your life? Besides, what do you know about leading a group?"

(**You** stay silent for a second or two and then move to the empty chair.)

A: "What makes you think I cannot lead a group? This is the moment I have been waiting for for so long. I will be able to learn and to mingle with extraordinary people, and my salary will be significantly higher."

The conversation goes on. Usually the emotional state of each character is noticeably different. **Me** only interrupts if there is a long silence that he (or she) interprets as a need for guidance. **Me** might ask one of the characters to change places. He can even ask either **A** or **B** to ask a specific question, or say something, or take some action that will make the conversation regain a lost momentum in **Me**'s view.

During the conversation **A** and **B** will get a clearer picture of what is happening to the other observer. This new knowledge of facts and feelings makes each of the observers more empathic, more able to place themselves in the other's situation. In almost all of the innumerable cases in which I have been **Me** in such a conversation, it has ended with a compromise between the two characters. **B** generally tries to defend **you** from failure. **A** gets into a mood of excitement that is able to seduce **B** into accepting not to interfere unless **A** asks her to.

I hope you now have the available resources for discovering who your observers are and what beliefs sabotage your intentions. I strongly recommend you do the exercise of finding within you those observers who contradict each other and have conversations like the one you just read in order to be clear on who you want to be, where you want to go, and how you want to get there. Doing this exercise repeatedly brings about a greater knowledge of yourself and drives you closer to your soul and purpose, whether defining them or becoming ready for the heart-centered journey towards them.

Another exercise that is useful in exploring the observers that you are is to close your eyes, relax your body, and visualize with closed eyes a situation in which one of your observers participates. This exercise will help you to know in a deeper way who and how the particular observer is.

Exploring your observers allows you to find your deepest beliefs, who and what you want to be, how some of your beliefs sabotage you, and how you can become the whole person you want to be.

Seeing myself through my different observers has been a very useful way to find my light and my shadows, my beliefs that are useful and the ones that are damaging, my most frequent moods and emotions, and my conditionings.

Observing your observers allows you to discover your purpose in life and what transformations you need to go through in order to fulfill it. Having that knowledge is essential for you to decide what you need to learn, and where and who to ask for help so that the learning will take place.

CHAPTER 6

Your Divine Gifts

Receiving and Returning

One of the first existential questions I remember asking as a young girl is "Why are we such complex and coordinated organisms, which allows us to do so much? Who could have conceived such organisms?" I could not answer that question, and nobody around me could give me a satisfying answer. I believed in the theory of evolution, but I could not understand through it the complexity of our bodies and their coordinated functionalities. I just stayed in awe, studying the encyclopedia, which showed our organs and functions in a schematic way. People of faith have a name for our Creator, which is totally acceptable for them. At any rate, religious or not, it is inevitable for me to think that the conception and design of the human body transcends the possibilities of our species. You can even observe the workings of this statement in the sequence in which technology has been developed. In the last century, for instance, technological development imitated the conception, design, and operation of machines. In the twenty-first century, we no longer talk about mechanisms, but now we talk about organisms. If we follow the development of robots, artificial intelligence, communication technology, animal cloning, and other creations, they all seem to be increasingly following a biological pattern. To me it seems formidable and scary at the same time. The universe has gifts for us that can be used for the good and also for the bad. This provides me with a sense of urgency to change the trend from "the bad" to "the good," which I am certain can be learned.

Nature itself can be considered a gift. The air we breathe, the soil that provides us food, the mountains, and the sea are all wondrous entities. Our bodies are amazing, as are many of their components such as our brains, hearts, lungs, bellies, and genitals. What these components can do and what they can create in association with others are also gifts. We can hear, see, smell, taste, touch, listen, imagine, visualize, perceive, analyze, talk, interpret, feel, and make choices. I find the gift of silence particularly inviting.

- Close your eyes for a couple of minutes in silence and visualize the gifts you have received.
- After a while, check how you are feeling.

- Open your eyes and write down all the gifts you can remember visualizing during this exercise.

Our Three Graces, **Will, Attention**, and **Discipline,** are gifts that we receive to make better lives for ourselves. You have probably discovered by now many of your strengths. Every one of them is a gift the universe brings to you. Being vulnerable and responsible are wonderful gifts, which we are often reluctant to take and use because of the internal observers who are in custody of our conditioned beings. Men have been taught that they must always be strong. Only women can allow themselves to sometimes be vulnerable. Becoming responsible instead of a victim of your circumstances will take you out of your comfort zone, and fear will arise, supplied by the observer who is there to defend you against the unknown and its dangers.

The possibility of relating to others, learning, and creating are also gifts. Look at the list you made in the exercise above. Add these gifts and see how many you have been given. I have no doubt that the number will be surprising, despite the fact that you might have left several behind.

When you thought about your life, did you take into consideration that you have been given all these gifts? If you didn't, it is time for you to start looking at the glass as being half full and also to work seriously on discovering your strengths; that is, blending what you know how to do well with loving it at the same time.

I invite you to be aware of the gifts you have received and of your strengths, and to discover the potential they bring to your life. Since your strengths are related to your passions, it is reasonable to think that your purpose in life has to do with all or some of them. If you are experiencing difficulties in discovering what you are meant to be and do in your life, go back to your strengths and discover your greatest passion. Stay with it for some days. Cuddle it and observe it in action. Have no doubt that you will start hearing a voice or you will feel something new that drives you into a different territory towards which you will feel a deep sense of attraction and belonging. You might want to check what Seligman names *character virtues and strengths*,[19] which you read about in chapter 4.

The universe provides you with many gifts, and there are also many that you can return to the universe. St. Paul said:

"Everything is shown up by being exposed to the light, and whatever is exposed to the light itself becomes light."[20]

You receive and you give, you receive and you give, in a continuous cycle.

While watching a taped workshop led by the late Debbie Ford some years ago, I heard her say something that still resonates in my ears, my heart, and my whole body:

"Where there is no love, put love there, and it will convert it to love."[21]

---

19. http://www.viacharacter.org/www/Character-Strengths/VIA-Classification
20. Ephesians 5:13, American Standard Bible.
21. Debbie Ford, inspirational speaker and bestselling transformational author

It works. I have tried it.

In the midst of World War II, Sir Winston Churchill made the 1941 commencement speech at Harrow School where he had studied in his youth. He said:

"Never give in. Never give in. Never, never, never, never—in nothing, great or small, large or petty—never give in, except to convictions of honor and good sense."[22]

Perseverance under any circumstance is a strength Churchill managed to develop, and he presented it as the most important strength of a decision-maker. The gift of perseverance allows decision-makers to return to the universe the gifts that they, in turn, received from it.

Stephen Hawking, the renowned and prized physicist and author who suffers from a severe muscular disease, said:

"However difficult life may seem, there is always something you can do and succeed at."[23]

Hawking teaches that no matter how difficult your life is, if you believe in yourself you will find the way to do what you want to do and be successful at it. He knows.

I heard Marshall Goldsmith, one of the most prestigious coaches in the world and a bestselling author, say in his series

---

22. http://content.time.com/time/specials/packages/article/0,28804,1898670_1898671_1898655,00.html
23. http://www.brainyquote.com/quotes/quotes/s/stephenhaw627103.html?src=t_success

"Leadership is a Contact Sport!":

"Treat the ideas that people give you as a gift. Thank them every time and use them when you consider it appropriate." [24]

Anytime you sense a chance for learning, take it as a gift. It might include the acknowledgment of a weakness you have, and the process might bring some discomfort to you; but if what you learn is worthy, you will acquire a new strength. You will have taken a step towards your fulfillment; and more so, if you teach what you learned you will be returning to the universe the gift it gave you.

I cannot leave the issue of learning without offering you an extremely important distinction. By learning I do not mean receiving information, even if you can reproduce it perfectly. In this book we shall consider learning as a process that results in your being able to do effectively something you were not capable of doing before, or improving your performance and results in a certain field.

Teaching, therefore, is not only instructing, but also requires you to help your students live the experience of going from point A to B and being able to perform what was impossible before, or to improve performance and results in a certain area. As a teacher you will have to ensure that your student is able to repeat their good performance at any time. I call this "recurring effectiveness." You will also need to ensure that they are autonomous in the specific learning and will not require

---

24. Marshall Goldsmith, "Leadership Is a Contact Sport": https://www.youtube.com/watch?v=ZcKiBRs6kVI

your help or anybody else's for their good performance in the stated area.

The Greatest Gift of All: Finding Meaning in Your Life

None of what has been written so far would have any relevance at all if it were not rooted in a sacred gift that has been given to our species. The world is here to provide us with meaning, with a sense of why or what we are here for.

Dr. Viktor Frankl is considered the master of masters in our "search for meaning." In fact, his autobiography, *Man's Search for Meaning*, has been read by millions and quoted by thousands. In the preface to the 1984 edition he tells us, when asked by a reporter how he felt about his book having become a bestseller:

> *"I see in the bestseller status of my book an expression of the misery of our time: if hundreds of thousands of people reach out for a book whose very title promises to deal with the question of a meaning to life, it must be a question that burns under their fingernails."* [25]

Let me add that the book was written in 1945 and published in 1959, 1962, and 1984, the latter being when Frankl made the comment written above. Apparently the question about the meaning of life is resistant to change.

---

25. V. Frankl, *Man's Search for Meaning*, Washington Square Press, 1984.

This question is related to personal freedom, which we have already dealt with in the introduction to this book when you read about the enormous amount of freedom we have, albeit limited by our environmental conditioning and our biological structure. Frankl refers to a very specific kind of freedom that might be considered the root of our lives.

Frankl lost almost all his family in the death camps in Europe, and having stayed in two of them himself for more than three years, he discovered that we have one freedom that cannot be taken away from us: the freedom to choose. He realized that we can choose and need to be responsible for who we want to be despite the worst conditions in which we may live. He defines despair as suffering without meaning. If you have something to live by and for, then you will be able to turn your suffering into achievement in terms of why or what you are living for.

Frankl also acknowledged that we cannot have absolute freedom. He said that we are limited to conditions—psychological, sociological, or political—that restrict it. Nevertheless, we do have what he calls the ultimate freedom: the way in which we react to our conditions is up to each one of us. In other words, if we cannot change our conditions, we do have the last freedom of changing our attitude towards those conditions.

While living subhumanly at the death camps, Frankl discovered what he called the true meaning of love when he visualized his wife, whom he knew nothing about while at the camp. (He later found out she had been murdered together with his and her parents.) He saw her vividly through his mind and had long imaginary conversations with her, which made him immensely happy. And his love for her never died.

Frankl turned his suffering into achievement after the war, finding himself all alone in Vienna. He created a therapeutic school that he named Logotherapy, dedicated to help people find meaning in their lives. In 1947 he remarried, and later became the father of a girl, Gabrielle.

Frankl's teachings, his therapies, and his influence in a world grasping for some semblance of meaning were readily listened to, not only after World War II but also in the second half of the twentieth century, and they continue to be highly influential today.

One of his students at Berkeley once posited, "... so this is your meaning in life ... to help others find meaning in theirs." His reply was: "That was it, exactly. Those are the very words I had written."[26]

This incredible man had lived in hell, so he had the authority to help people in the gravest of situations. But sometimes people fail to find meaning in any kind of situation in life. Probably these people do not know that they can learn to look at the glass as half full and define their own path.

Is meaning important in your life? If so, this book is meant for you. I will do whatever is in my reach to show you that it is possible to reverse your natural tendency towards the bad, and hopefully transform the attitude with which you might be looking at life and its circumstances. This will be your starting point towards fulfillment.

---

26. V. Frankl, *Recollections: An Autobiography*, Kindle Edition, August 2008

Leadership guru John Maxwell tells us:

"In life, the question is not if you will have problems, but how you are going to deal with your problems.[27]"

In other words, it is certain that you will have to cope with problems. The issue here is what your attitude regarding them will be. It is worthwhile to remember Frankl's words: "Whatever the conditions of your life are, you have the freedom to choose what your attitude will be."

Maxwell offers us an important exercise that he learned at a young age:

"Suppose you cannot fail. You will meet some problems but you will not fail. If this were the case, what would you attempt to achieve?" [28]

I invite you to reflect, to dream, to visualize the answer, and respond to this simple but not easy question.

As a coach I have experienced the difficulty that some of my clients have had in finding meaning in their lives. This has led me to think that the issue of meaning is probably one of the main reasons for human suffering. You can choose to make yourself responsible and turn your suffering into your ally, as proposed by Frankl, or else you can stay where you are, even if you are not enjoying your place and your stay, and be

---
27. https://www.goodreads.com/quotes/691712
28. http://www.johnmaxwell.com/blog/stop-thinking-can-i-and-start-thinking-how-can-i

a victim of circumstance. The choice is up to you. My offer is to help you become who you want to be and experiment with fulfillment, to which you are 100% entitled, provided you take responsibility for the path you will take.

The issue of meaning connects me to a greater space than the ordinary, and I tend to approach the ineffable mystery of the world. So I will say no more for now, and we shall leave this chapter with the following questions:

- Have you been provided with gifts?
- What are the ones you treasure most?
- Have you given gifts back to life?
- What are they?

CHAPTER 7

The Body-Emotion-Language Connection

Being and Acting

In the former chapter you were invited to think about and write down what other gifts you have received from the universe apart from the ones that were noted there. I truly hope you included the ones we are going to explore in this chapter, since they are basic elements of the work we shall be doing later on. They will allow you to create a heart-centered path for fulfillment. These three gifts are **body, emotions, and language** (human language). You will see how these elements contribute to making you the human being that you are, how they relate to each other, and the importance of that relationship in your actions.

Your actions constitute your behavior, and your behavior provides your identity, which shows who you are, including all your internal observers, the observer of your observers, and your soul, as shown in chapter 5. In turn, your soul is the being you are, the one who acts or behaves. At the same time your actions turn you into who you are, so your being is not separate from your actions. As said, who you are being determines what your actions are. Nevertheless, new actions and behaviors change your identity. There is a continuous connection between being and behaving.

Modifying, creating, or eliminating a behavior can turn you into a different person who is able to act in new ways. If you learn how to eliminate harmful behaviors and create new, healthier ones, you will become the person you want to be and the leader of your life. You will gain the capacity to decide where you want to go and to design the path to get there.

This dynamic will take place only if you use one of the gifts already mentioned: your freedom, or your capacity to choose. Please answer the following questions and explore beneath the surface of your body and the actions you perform:

- Do I believe I can choose?
- Can I choose my behavior?
- Can I change my behavior?
- Will I become a different being if I change my behavior?

I suggest you write down these questions and post them in various places where you can be sure to see them on a regular basis. You do not need to answer them. Just contemplate the questions and see how your body reacts. Check to see if an emotion arises, and name it. Do this exercise as often as possible. Say each question out loud and see how your body and emotional being respond. As I stated, do not answer them at this time.

Our Three Graces, **Will, Attention,** and **Discipline,** will help you concentrate on doing this exercise. You might learn something about beliefs and feelings that show up that you never thought you had.

Observing Yourself and Others in Action

Imagine you are walking in the street towards the building where you have a business meeting in twenty minutes. You are walking slowly and somewhat distractedly because you are very near and do not want to arrive ahead of time.

A woman crosses the street and inadvertently bumps into you. After a few seconds, when you recover from the surprise, you look at her, undecided whether to talk to her or just keep walking. The woman is also recovering from the incident. You notice that she is wearing a shabby coat, her hair looks unkempt, and her shoulders are slumped. You look at her face and suddenly recognize her. She is your classmate Amanda, whom you have not seen for at least a decade. You gently touch her arm and say,

You: "Hello Amanda, what a surprise to see you!"

Amanda stops and looks at you very briefly. Then she lowers her head and says, without looking at you and in a very low tone of voice,

A: "Oh, how funny, I almost knocked you over without realizing it was you. It is so nice to see you. You made my day. It's really great."

You: "I am also happy to see you. How are you?"

Amanda still does not look at you. Her eyes are slanted and almost shut, and her lips are sealed in a grimace. You cannot help feeling sad for her. After a few seconds Amanda replies, without lifting her face or her tone of voice.

A: "Oh, I am fine. I couldn't be better. I am married, with two children. I am not working now because they still need me at home. Life is fun. How are you?"

You: "I am fine, too. And actually, I need to leave because I have to rush to a meeting right now. So long, Amanda, be well!"

A: "Sure. Bye now. It was marvelous to see you."

You leave, feeling uneasy.

THE BODY-EMOTION-LANGUAGE CONNECTION

> - What is the first thing you noticed about Amanda?
> - What made you feel uneasy?
> - What was your impression of Amanda?

The first thing you notice when you meet someone is the way their body manifests its presence. If you believed Amanda when she said she was having fun in her life, in spite of her worn-out appearance, slanting eyes, sealed lips, and monotonous voice, you will probably say to yourself something like "She needs to work on her physical appearance. Her presence is totally unappealing. Maybe she is ill?"

That is always the sequence in which we see others. We first notice presence, body postures, facial movement, and other nonverbal signals such as tone of voice, eye contact, gestures, and position of shoulders.

Presence also reveals the condition of your health and your attitude in life. Your haircut and color, and the way you dress in a certain environment, can reveal a compliant or a defiant attitude in regard to certain codes of etiquette. I remember having a managerial position in my late twenties and refusing to accept the standard dress code. I wore tight jeans and light Indian blouses. This caused me to be summoned by my boss. He told me that my way of dressing was unacceptable for a manager, and that I would never gain respect from my collaborators. I understood the importance of codes and conventions much later in life.

Besides perceiving a person's presence, you will sense their emotional state. In fact, the body helps a great deal in expressing emotions. Amanda's body posture when she greeted you suggested deep sadness. Her words were trying to convey the opposite, but I believed her body and not her words. My conclusion was that her words were not expressing the truth. If you sensed the sad or gloomy connection between the body and the emotions, you probably also said to yourself, "What she is saying is not true." However, Amanda probably thought her words sufficed to let you know that she was happy. Nevertheless, you surely listened to how unhappy she was.

Amanda's body and emotions might have been aligned, but her language was not. Inevitably, in this case, you will believe the combination of presence and feelings as the truth, and you will judge her words as untrue.

Lack of awareness of the precedence of presence and emotions in regard to language can become the beginning of an unfortunate story of bad communication.

Emotions and feelings happen. They reveal themselves in our tone of voice, our posture, and our degree of bodily relaxation. You must learn to identify them, since they define possible and impossible actions. For example, if you are feeling deeply grateful at a given time, surely it will not be the right moment to fire someone from your team.

THE BODY-EMOTION-LANGUAGE CONNECTION

- Remember the last time you felt angry.
- Would you have been able to declare your love to your significant other at that moment?

You can modify a mood or emotion by doing something with your body. Through changes in body postures and movements you can change an emotion. For example, if you like aerobics, you can get rid of your anger by practicing it. If you want to get rid of your feeling of sadness, you can dance.

You can also use language to change what you are feeling right now. For instance, you can tell someone why you are angry, and they might help you change your mood with a little bit of humor or capture your attention by telling you something they know will interest you. Or you can write poetry. Just use your imagination and your known strengths. If you practice, it will become easy for you to change a mood by using your body or language as tools.

Body, emotions, and language are all present and important in our actions and communication with ourselves and others. As a matter of fact, only through language can each of us find meaning in our lives. It is human language that distinguishes our human species from other animals. All animals have bodies and emotions. Only humans have the type of language that can create new realities and connect us to the meaning and the mystery of life.

What I am trying to express here is that our bodies, our presence, and our emotions, moods, and feelings are inextricable components of our actions, behaviors, conversations, and relationships. They precede the action of speech, creating a context that enables or disables possible actions. As important as verbal language is, a fulfilled person never forgets or neglects their body and their feelings. These three gifts are always present during their life journey.

Aligning Body, Emotions, and Language in Conversations

You are probably realizing at this point how different it is to act in the world with our bodies, emotions, and language coherently connected as opposed to expressing different things with your body than with your words. If there is a contradiction between your presence and your verbal language, people will believe what you are expressing with your body rather than what you are expressing with your words. That is why it is crucial for actors to learn how to adapt their physical movements and tones of voice to the text and the emotions the playwright or the director wants to convey to the audience. A stiff body conveys only the emotions that a stiff body can show.

The following story allows us to understand how body, emotions, and language dance together in a working environment.

Samuel is the chief programmer of the application Schedint, a scheduling automated manager. He is in charge of a group of three less-senior programmers. Samuel is used to talking to peers, and, in general, to people with a technical background, in his daily activities. In fact, the relationships he has established with his collaborators are similar to the ones he developed with his direct boss and with chief programmers of other applications in the same company. Samuel feels comfortable and relaxed with all these people. They even go out for a beer together from time to time.

On the other hand, Samuel seldom speaks to Alan, who is the owner and CEO of the company. They greet each other at the Christmas party that the company hosts each year for the employees, and this basically summarizes their level of communication. Alan speaks to Samuel's boss about issues related to the latter's area, not to Samuel. Actually, Samuel is beginning to notice that his stomach hurts every time he feels an obligation to approach the CEO. If you asked him how he is feeling at that moment, he would reply that he feels anxious. In spite of feeling pain and anxiety, Samuel does not pay attention to his stomach or to his emotions. He is used to them and does not think those symptoms will ever go away. He does focus on finding the right words so that he can prove to Alan that he is intelligent and competent.

As for the sales department, although Samuel knows he should speak to the salespeople, he avoids it. It is difficult for him to relate to them. His body gets stiff and he usually feels pressure in his neck and head when he has to meet the sales manager or anyone from the sales department. He has heard comments from sales executives complaining that programmers are difficult people, square and rigid. At the same time, Samuel has complained to his boss that the salespeople are scoundrels who sell things that do not yet exist.

Here is a conversation between Samuel and Ralf, the collaborator he works most intensely with:

R: "Hi boss, are you coming from the meeting with the sales manager?"
S: "Yes. Who told you I was there?"
R: "Nobody told me. It's just that your face is red. You look agitated and angry. So where else could you possibly have come from?"
S: "I am NOT angry!"
R: "Sorry, Samuel, I didn't mean to annoy you. Anyway, I was waiting for you. May I show you the presentation draft?"

When Samuel came into his office, the first thing that Ralf noticed was Samuel's red face and his agitated state. He interpreted his boss's presence and feelings as anger and stress.

- Did you believe Samuel when he said he was not angry?
- Was there body-emotions-language alignment in Samuel?
- If the behavior and judgments among the different groups in the company persist, what could happen?

The distance the CEO establishes with the technical groups, the mutual prejudices between the programming and sales departments, and the physical discomfort that Samuel feels when he meets the CEO or the salespeople have left him somewhat orphaned from communication. He only knows what is happening in the company through his direct boss or from rumors that sometimes circulate.

- Will it be easy for Samuel to grow professionally in this company?
- Is it important to converse in the company?
- Does Samuel have conversations?
- If he has conversations, what is the quality of Samuel's conversations?
- If you were Samuel, what would you do to improve your position in the company?

The extent of your world is determined by your experience; your early conditioning; the various observers who make you the being you are, known and hidden beliefs included; and the quality of the relationships that you have made through your experience.

You express yourself in conversations with yourself and others through your body, your emotions, your feelings, your thoughts, and the words that are said by those who are participating in the conversation. You have seen that a conversation is much more than merely words.

Becoming aware of the need for body-emotions-language alignment is the first step in understanding what conversations are and the power they can bring to you while travelling your path for fulfillment. This means that what you say with words must be aligned with what your body shows and with what you are feeling. I suggest you remind yourself of the need for this alignment in every conversation you consider important or difficult. This will happen with practice and repetition.

- In your next conversation, observe how congruent your body and feelings are with what you say. Remember to observe your body, then your emotions, and finally determine if your words are in harmony with them.
- Now observe the body, emotions, and words of the person with whom you are having the conversation.
- Did you observe something new? If so, what?

CHAPTER 8

Incubation of PEL-MET

What Your Body Can Show You

Several years ago, I was having a coaching session with my client Anita. Suddenly she became silent, and after a while she exclaimed, "There are serious issues in my life that I really need to overcome!"

We stayed silent a little longer, and then she said, as if she were talking to herself, "I have always thought of myself as a very normal human being living the life I am supposed to live, with some ups and downs, but nothing special. I now realize that underneath the surface all is chaos, and I feel an urgent need to start from scratch!"

This was the moment in which we could really start a transformational process.

Anita had come to me through a referral, as do most of my clients, three months before her "Aha" exclamation. She wanted to have a few conversations with a coach who could help her clarify her professional aspirations. She did not feel comfortable at her present job and felt she lacked clarity about what she wanted concerning her professional life. That was all the help she felt she needed.

Although we had had conversations and practiced some exercises so that she would experience the body-emotions-language alignment, Anita had not yet fully grasped it in depth.

On this particular day, while we were working on her physical sensations, she suddenly realized that she was not only confused about her job preferences, but actually her whole life came into question. For the first time she became aware that her marriage was not working, understood that her parents had had a negative influence in her life, was not sure that she was being the kind of mother she wanted to be for her two children, and saw herself wasting energy by anxiously competing in her mind with her professional friends. She even questioned her value as a person.

After throwing out words without stopping for quite a while, she looked suffocated and said, in a choked voice, "My whole body hurts, and I have difficulty breathing!"

Despite how disturbed Anita seemed to be, I did not do anything other than breathe normally while calmly saying to her, "Just look at me and concentrate on how I am breathing."

Anita squirmed in her chair, and I could feel her discomfort. I invited her to get up and walk around the room if she felt like it, and then come back, every so often, to see how I was breathing. Slowly she calmed down and sat in her chair again. Once more I asked her to watch me breathe. When I realized that she was not so upset any longer, I asked her to breathe with me, to emulate my breathing pattern. In fact, I started to breathe at Anita's rhythm for a couple of minutes until her face became placid and I could see she had calmed down.

This was not the first time I had mirrored one of my client's breathing. I had tried this exercise many times and it had already become a coaching resource for me. It was very useful for getting my clients out of painful emotions and into a state of relaxation. This new state creates openness to a visualizing exercise. The client feels more at ease, enabling space for self-exploration and discovery.

The exercise is triggered either by the client expressing their displeasure or by my realizing that at a certain point there is no room for verbal conversation. I say softly that we will interrupt our discussion for a while and then I ask the client to check if they are having a distinct sensation in their body that was not present before. Usually the client easily recognizes a physical pressure or pain in a specific place in their body without difficulty. I then ask the client to concentrate on that sensation and explore if there is movement, or a change in intensity. After one minute I ask them to direct their attention to their breathing until they recover their normal rhythm.

You can see that in Anita's case I started right away with the action of breathing. I considered that her physical reaction had been addressed by her awareness that it had become difficult for her to breathe.

After the session I felt the urge to summarize this coaching experience in writing. Anita and I had not talked about emotions, but nevertheless I felt the whole session was intensely emotional. Besides, the exercise of abruptly focusing her attention on the body suddenly became a very clear signal that at that moment it was necessary for her to get as far away as possible from any verbal expression.

I realized that I had found a starting point for igniting a process that is triggered by directing your attention to a new bodily sensation, no matter how dim it is, as soon as it arises. Then you need to pay attention to your breathing and get it back to your normal rhythm. When your body is calm and you are breathing at your normal frequency, your heart will pump the blood it receives from and to your lungs in its normal capacity. Thus you become calm and heart-centered.

It became clear to me that this method would consist of a precise sequence of stages. I knew that first of all we need to address our body, which is not necessarily an automatic process. We need some education in order to be able to perform the first two steps. First we need to practice (repeat) the exercise of becoming alert to our body sensations. Next we must discover what our normal breathing pattern is and how to obtain it. The way to do this is to repeat the exercise of putting all your attention on your breathing. Your breathing will probably then relax, which helps you calm down. You might need some help if your body is a relatively unexplored territory. Imitating someone else's rhythm can help.

Anita's situation had become highly emotional. Nevertheless, the substance of the method I was developing was to find an observer of the observers of Anita's body. (Remember the metaphoric non-judgmental observer of the observers from chapter 5?) This observer would help her stick to watching her body and breathing, letting go of words and emotions. The first step of this method is addressing the body, even if you or the person you are with is enduring a highly emotional state. Creating the habit of quickly distinguishing a new physical sensation, identifying it without words, visualizing it, and then putting all your attention on your breathing can be difficult if you are not prepared to repeat the process as many times as needed. This exercise can be tricky, especially when you are unaware of your tendency to stick to your emotions or to have your mind filled with words. So should you have some difficulty repeating this exercise successfully, I suggest you ask for help in order to learn how to create the habit. You will know you have mastered it when you can to turn your attention to your body automatically, without help, over and over again.

Clients who have been successful in turning these first two steps into a habit have also enjoyed discovering surprisingly hidden aspects that are displayed when they put their attention on their body. A whole new world opened for Anita when she decided to repeat, repeat, and repeat these first two steps. Later on, she worked on the whole method, until she could happily show me what it meant for her to have turned it into a habit.

The Role of Habits

Habits are repeated, automatic behaviors. Your life and mine are full of them. We are conscious of some and not of others. Some are useful to the extent that if we did not practice them on a daily basis, life could be very demanding and busier than we could handle; others can be harmful or unhealthy. We might not even be aware of some of them since they are probably consequences of hidden beliefs that we may not even know we have.

We create our habits from the materials we use in our daily lives, such as experiences, information, beliefs, thoughts, emotions, bodily sensations, conditioning, and the presence that we show to the world around us.

- Make a list of your known habits and judge them as useful, undesirable, or neutral.
- Explore possible unknown habits by observing yourself and asking people you trust. Make a list and judge them as useful, undesirable, or neutral.
- Did you learn something about yourself from this exercise?

PEL-MET Is Born

When Anita was able to turn the two steps into a habit, I knew that a new system had been born, which I later called PEL-MET.

INCUBATION OF PEL-MET

STEP 1:
a. Pay attention to a new physical sensation as soon as it arises.
b. Abruptly cease any activity you are doing.
c. Identify the new sensation without words.
d. Visualize the new sensation.

STEP 2:
a. Register your normal breathing frequency.[29] (Only once, for use as a possible reference.)
b. Focus your attention on your present breathing frequency.
c. Visualize yourself at your normal breathing frequency or follow someone else's breathing rhythm.
d. Observe the reduction of your breathing frequency until it is normal.
e. Observe your normal rhythm for one or two minutes.

The Why, How, and What of PEL-MET

I want to share with you how this name came to be. MET simply stands for *method* in English and Spanish; PEL stands for presence, emotions, and language in English, and *presencia, emociones,* and *lenguaje* in Spanish. I wanted to create a name that was identical in English and Spanish since these are the two languages I mostly use in my profession, and I think I can reach as many people as possible with them.

---

29. This registration is to be used only as a reference in Step 2 of PEL-MET. It is invalid for medical purposes. When calm, resting, and lying down, count the number of times your chest rises in one minute.

You have seen the importance of aligning body, emotions, and language. Unfortunately "body" does not start with the same letter in both languages (*cuerpo* in Spanish). I had to find a similar word, or one that relates to it.

I found it. Presence is what our bodies show to the outside world. It is an essential component in our communication with others. Your presence is a key element of the impression you make on others.

PEL-MET was out there, waiting to be discovered. It was a hidden gift the universe had given us. The only thing I did was find the tip of the strand and hold it, letting it slip through my fingers while it showed me the path. PEL-MET is a simple set of precise steps you can take when you are feeling uncomfortable, no matter the source of discomfort. You might feel lost concerning what your purpose in life is. You might not be getting the results you want in a scientific experiment you are undertaking. You might feel that something is not going in the right direction during an important conversation or a less important one, or you might be wondering how to start a conversation with your boss about a salary raise that will not come if you do not take the initiative and ask.

Regardless of the dimension of your challenge, PEL-MET is a simple method that when turned into a habit provides you with sensors that check your presence-emotions-language alignment and allows you to correct it in a very short time. You do not need to interrupt what you are doing to realign these three very basic elements that reveal the person you are being at any given time.

INCUBATION OF PEL-MET

The reason I needed to create PEL-MET, in other words my WHY, is that I am a catalyzer of awareness, fulfillment, and, ultimately, transformation. In order to get any of these results, you must first be aligned. What you express with your body has to be in harmony with your emotions, and the words you speak must, in turn, harmonize with them. I take the sequence Why-How-What from the ideas expressed by Simon Sinek.[30] By the way, starting with "Why" and not with "What" helps you better understand your purpose and calling in life. I have always asked my students, my clients, the people I work with, and myself, "What is your reason for doing this?" I perceive this question as equivalent to Sinek's "Why," since in both cases we are envisioning the future.

My HOW is to reveal my WHY through a simple and repetitive method with the potential of creating a habit. If you acquire the automatic behavior of practicing PEL-MET in any given circumstance, you will reach a certain goal or you will be honoring a purpose you declared. Certainly you need to know what the goal or the purpose of your actions is. By using this method repetitively and in the right sequence, the presence-emotions-language alignment will be generated even if you are not aware of it, and it will turn you into a heart-centered person. If you know where you want to go, this method will act as a compass to help you travel in the direction of fulfillment.

The WHAT is the sequence of steps that must be taken, always in the same order, creating a specific behavior that can

---

30. Simon Sinek, *Start with Why*, Penguin Books, 2009.

become a habit if the sequence is repeated as many times as needed in order for it to be performed automatically.

Discovering PEL-MET through Experience

Anita had the direct experience of changing her emotional state by concentrating on breathing. The first time she performed this exercise it probably did not make much sense to her. Thankfully she respected me as a coach and gave me the authority to lead her into the exercise. She did not know what it was for, what she could learn from it, or how it could impact her in any way. She made the effort to breathe the same way I was breathing, but at first she could not feel my rhythm. Hers was quicker than her normal rhythm. As she was walking around the room, she inadvertently started to calm down, and while doing so she regained her normal breathing frequency. When she sat down I followed her rhythm for a while, leading her to peace. This could only happen if she concentrated solely on her breathing. My role was to help her reach that level of concentration.

The aim of this exercise is to abruptly stop the internal conversations that you might be having. You have already seen that these internal conversations can lead you out of the "here and now," leaving you with no presence at all regarding the people around you or the person you are having a conversation with.

Anita and I agreed that during the week she would be attentive to sensations coming from her body. She told me that in the past she had identified temple beats, a contraction of the muscles that surround the vocal cords, arrhythmia, and blushing.

Preparing Yourself for PEL-MET

Sit comfortably on a chair with your feet parallel to each other, completely touching the floor without pressing down on it. You can use softly playing music for relaxation.

- Close your eyes and slowly visualize your body, starting with the toes and going up along the front of your body very slowly. Let go of any tension you might feel during this journey.
- When you get to the top of your head, start slowly visualizing the back side of your body until you reach your toes. Again, let go of any tension you find on the way.
- Finally, quickly check if there is still tension in any part of your body, and let go of it.
- How do you feel?

This exercise is not a part of PEL-MET. It is a very simple, well-known exercise that allows you to become relaxed and open to aligning your body with your emotions. I recommend you repeat it often, since a heart-centered person requires the habit of relaxing. When you master this practice, you will see that you need less and less time to relax. Eventually, if you learn to relax fast enough, you might want to include this exercise as a prologue to PEL-MET. You are very welcome to do so!

PEL-MET has a wider purpose. It should allow you to align presence, emotions, and language, without significantly interrupting your present activity, whether it is a conversation you are having, a meeting you are attending, or a speech you are giving to an audience. This means that concentrating on your sensations first and on your breathing next has to be done automatically in order to be as fast as the situation demands. You need to create a habit of concentrating on your body and your breathing.

My recommendation is to practice these two (or three if you include the previous relaxation exercise) steps until they are effortless. When this happens, you will be ready to learn PEL-MET Step 3.

CHAPTER 9

Getting Ready for PEL-MET, Step 3

Connecting Body and Emotions

Anita spent several months practicing, and sometimes forgetting to practice, Steps 1 and 2 of PEL-MET. I think it is helpful to remember that deliberately getting rid of or creating a new habit is not a natural and easy thing to do. As said, every one of us has many habits. They are automatic behaviors and we do not realize that we have most of them since they are unconsciously acquired through genetics, conditioning, and early influences from various environmental sources.

In chapter 4 you identified your strengths, and in chapter 6 you probably discovered the most significant gifts the universe has to offer. The significant gifts plus your strengths provide you with many of the needed tools to become heart-centered and find a path for fulfillment. When Anita and my other clients worked together, this book did not exist, so we co-created PEL-MET by performing exercises and observing what happened. I owe it to you and the rest of the readers of this book to make your life easier by providing you with a systematic and tested method. Thank you, Anita, and all the clients and students who helped me put this system in place!

One day after Anita told me that she was starting to feel comfortable and aware of her breathing, we had the following conversation:

Me: "Anita, what has happened to you since we started our conversations?"

A: "You know, Sally, although I am not one-hundred-percent happy about my will power and discipline, I can really observe my learning. And I feel great about it!"

Me: "May I give you a hug, Anita? In these few sentences, I listened to three wonderful things about you that are new to me. First, you can observe your learning. This means that you can detach yourself from your own actions and observe the observer who is learning.

"Second, you are also saying that you have embodied the distinction of learning. In other words, you are aware of doing something effectively, as many times as you wish, and you don't need help.

"And the third thing, which is very important, is that you like yourself. Did you really express these three things?"

Anita was silent for a moment. She seemed to be reflecting on what I had just said. Finally she stood up, gave me a nice big hug, and returned to her seat.

A: "I wouldn't go as far as saying, 'I like myself.' I do like myself sometimes. And I think I can learn to like myself more spontaneously. Actually, I dream about the day when I will be able to look at myself in the mirror and not need to fake that I like myself. I really do! Thinking that this day will come fills me with joy and peace."

Me: "Do you realize, Anita, how far you have travelled into the space of awareness of who you can be and what you can do, just by repeating over and over again the two steps that deal with your presence, with your body?"

Anita's eyes opened wide and a surprised look came over her face. After a while she said,

A: "But Sally, we haven't said anything about the body in this conversation! What are you talking about?"

Me: "I believe we are talking about how you can affect your feelings and conversations by paying systematic attention to your body. You did not seem your old self when I listened to what you were just telling me. Knowing your body and using it purposefully has transformational powers. By the way, I suggest you look at your face in the bathroom mirror right now, okay?"

Anita rose quickly, smiled at me, and went into the bathroom to look at herself in the mirror. She did not come back right away. When she did, I asked her,

Me: "Did you see something interesting?"
A: "Amazing! I could not leave the mirror. My eyes were bright, my cheeks slightly red, and the smile on my face never disappeared. I even saw a pretty woman in there!"

Anita's breathing became faster after my question, and she seemed very alert. I remained silent, just watching her and sharing her delight. Suddenly she asked,

A: "Did I take too long?"
Me: "I did not feel that. I was also enjoying your experience. Have you noticed that joy is contagious?"

- Have you been joyful?
- What is joy for you?
- What possibilities does joy open?

Anita and I were referring to what we call emotions, feelings, and moods. Not all authors agree on the definitions of each of these words, so in the next section I propose my own in order to fulfill the purpose of this book.

For me, the purpose of this book is to widen your vision of what is possible for you and others in order to become the leader of your own life, surrendering to the innumerable gifts the universe provides, and becoming responsible for deciding where you want to go. I am providing you with many tools to undertake your journey towards fulfillment. PEL-MET is one of them. It is a method that allows you to align your body with your emotions, feelings, and moods, and with your verbal conversation. This alignment is the starting point of your path.

Emotions, Feelings, and Moods

Let us understand emotions as responses from your body to unexpected events generated in your environment that interrupt the transparency of your habitual life. It has been said that we are creatures of habit. Habits are automatic behaviors. We go through life in the transparency of our habits. I will give you an example:

David usually comes home from work on Fridays around 5:30 p.m. One Friday Rita, his wife, called him at 4:00 p.m. to tell him that she had left a marinated salmon steak in the fridge for his dinner. She also told David that she had bought fresh bread, vegetables, and fruit, and that the beer and white wine were already cold. Rita was ready to leave their apartment in Boston. She would spend the weekend with her friend Lily at Martha's Vineyard. Her friend had come to visit her parents there from her home in London, England. Rita told David that it would take her about three hours to get to Lily's parents' house.

While he was driving home, David sighed and daydreamed about enjoying his favorite meal and drinking to his heart's content while watching the local baseball match on his huge TV set. For him it was impossible to find a better way to end a stressful work week. He loved the idea of having a lot of food, drinks, and time for himself while his wife was having fun elsewhere. He arrived home as usual, without paying much attention to the traffic and the lights.

David parked the car in the underground parking lot of his building, got out, and headed towards the elevator while searching for his house key where he always kept it, in the outer pocket of his leather bag. He did not find it. He stopped and rummaged through the pocket with his fingers. No key. He looked inside the bag between the folders and personal items like pens and pencils, toothbrush, and sunglasses. Still there was no key.

By now David's breath was agitated and faster than normal. He opened the trunk of his car and poured out the entire contents of his leather bag. He shook the bag until there was nothing left inside it. Holding it with one hand, he took a few steps, shaking it and looking at the trunk from every possible angle. The key was not there. David sat back in his car. He was gasping for air while shaking his head from side to side. He heard himself saying out loud, "What am I going to do?" His face was hot and he felt sweat dripping from his temples.

What happened?

David had driven home in the transparency of a routine that had created a habit. He did not need to pay a lot of attention to his driving or even to the traffic around him to reach his destination. At a certain moment, the transparency of his routine was broken. David had a breakdown: the house key was not where it was supposed to be, and he needed it. From then on, everything changed. His body turned stiff, his breathing became agitated, and before he started rummaging through the bag he experienced an emotion. First he felt body sensations of which he might have been more or less aware. Then he experienced an emotion.

- Have you ever had an experience similar to the one David went through?
- Can you describe your body sensations when that happened?
- Did you experience an emotion(s)?
- If you did, what would you call the emotion(s) you felt at that time?
- What did you do physically, and what did you say after the breakdown?

I would call the emotion that got hold of David when he realized that the key was missing anxiety. He became very active trying to find that key. This activity was triggered by the emotion that held him. There was no thinking, no reflection. He engaged in an unconscious, frantic activity as if he had expected to find the key by means of it. The emotion grabbed him and conditioned his actions. He made some unconscious movements and did not take other actions such as thinking.

Emotions, feelings, and moods precede actions, allowing some types of actions to take place and inhibiting others. While David was experiencing deep anxiety, it probably would not have occurred to him to pick up the phone and ask for help.

The inexplicit and unconscious objective of finding the key was not met. David's body reacted again, and this time anxiety was replaced by another emotion when he went back and sat in the car.

- What emotion replaced anxiety in David's story?

I would say that when David returned to his car, rather than being simply anxious, he became paralyzed by fear, which is one of the ways in which we act unconsciously when we experience this emotion. Now that he was not busy, fear and the feeling of helplessness triggered his action in language when he asked, "What am I going to do?"

- How would you finish this story?
- Describe David's emotions in your part of the story

When David was driving home his mood was lively, as if he were thinking, *Life is good*. He anticipated the feeling of a pleasant state of relaxation. By the time he stopped searching for the house key, that feeling probably had changed to helplessness and a mood of frustration. He was surely not thinking that life is good anymore.

GETTING READY FOR PEL-MET, STEP 3

You can see here the presence of emotions, feelings, and moods. At the beginning of this section, I proposed how to distinguish an emotion:[31] a response from your body to an unexpected event generated in your environment that interrupts the transparency of your habitual life.

A mood is not created as a consequence of an unexpected event. It is the product of the combination of several factors and sources such as lifestyle, family conditioning, weather, social environment, geography, culture, and a series of emotions that you might have experienced in the past. It is a manifestation of how you perceive your life. Regardless of external events, you can have an optimistic mood or a pessimistic one. You can see the glass as half empty or half full. You can have a mood of enthusiasm or of stagnation, and you can accept the facts of life or resent them. Moods last longer than emotions. They can also be modified by an emotion for a period of time. Actually, depending on the impact of the emotion, the previous mood can reappear or it can be replaced by another mood.

A feeling usually combines physical sensations with our thinking about them. It contains a cognitive or linguistic aspect and is triggered by one or more emotions. Feelings last longer than emotions.

While David was driving home, his mood of liveliness almost created a feeling of relaxation. The mood and the feeling were disrupted by the emotions of anxiety and fear. Anxiety caused muscle contraction and body movement. Then the emotion of fear loosened the muscles and prevented body

---

31. For a more detailed explanation of the distinctions among emotions, feelings, and moods, visit http://www.6seconds.org/2015/01/02/emotion-feeling-mood

movement, which in turn created a feeling of helplessness. These emotions and feelings made the mood shift into frustration.

If you finished the story, you can keep track of the later emotional developments according to your interpretation. David must have found some solution, finally, and the emotion of fear must have vanished or been greatly reduced. The feeling of helplessness and the mood of frustration must have evolved according to how David felt about himself after solving the problem and how satisfied he was with the solution.

Body, emotional state (emotions, moods, feelings), and language (thought, cognition, and verbal conversation) are always present and constantly interacting. In order to build a path for fulfillment, they must be congruent and aligned. I do not think that David could have felt an emotion of joy when he realized he did not have his house key. That would have been inconsistent with his situation. His body couldn't relax when the emotion of anxiety overwhelmed him, and when he became able to think again, his thoughts were probably devoted to solving his problem.

PEL-MET is a method that allows you to deliberately find needed congruence and alignment. We have seen the effects of Steps 1 and 2, which deal with becoming aware of body presence and its alignment with a certain situation. The next step helps align body presence and emotional states.

PEL-MET, Step 3

As you might remember, the first action you need to take when executing PEL-MET is to detect a new physical sensation. The fact that it is new means that an event has happened and produced some sort of change. Now you can observe more keenly than before when the transparency of your life has been broken.

Earlier in this chapter you read that when this happens you can expect an emotion to disturb you in some way.

STEP 3:
a. Identify the emotion (or emotions) that are showing up in your body now.
b. Name it (or each one).

The action is verbal, and it consists only of naming. Use one word, and only one, for each emotion. Giving emotions names allows you to distinguish and clarify them.

You are ready to practice the relaxation exercise prior to performing PEL-MET Steps 1, 2, and 3. I highly recommend this repetitive practice before entering into the next steps.

CHAPTER 10

PEL-MET Verbal Steps

The first two steps of PEL-MET deal with your body presence, while the third step is meant to bring awareness of your emotions. The next two steps will create alignment of your body presence and emotions with your thinking and verbal expression.

Dreams and Desires; Purpose and Objectives

When Anita came to me, she perceived her life as that which she was supposed to live. She had a husband, a seven-year-old son, and was six months pregnant with a girl. They spent many weekends sharing meals with her sister, two brothers, and her parents.

Anita thought of herself as professionally competent and well-prepared for any managerial position. She had an MBA, liked to teach, and had a job at a local university. Her only problem was that she did not like the way the university was managed. Among other things, she was loaded down with administrative work instead of having the time to prepare her lessons and assist her students, and her salary was not the one she thought she deserved. Sometimes she met some fellow MBA classmates for a drink and did not speak a word. While they boasted about how interesting and well-paying their jobs were, she resented not being able to compete with them, although she had been a better student than several of them.

Anita seemed lively and had a beautiful smile. She insisted that her only problem was that she did not want to stay at her job after the baby was born and her pregnancy leave ended. She felt confused about what her working options were, and that is why she needed my help.

I asked her,

Me: "Anita, if you project yourself in time, let's say two years from now, what would you desire your working life to be like?"

Anita frowned and her facial expression stayed like that for a while. I did not speak either. She seemed perplexed by my question. Finally she said,

A: "I don't understand your question. I think I told you already. I want to have a good job where I can feel well and receive a decent salary."

Me: "What job would make you feel well and how much do you want to receive as a salary?"

This time there was no answer. It seemed Anita knew that she wanted to feel good about her job, including her monthly earnings, but apparently she had not figured out what that meant to her or how much money she really wanted.

We did a relaxation exercise, and then I asked her to visualize herself doing the work she wanted to do. Anita closed her eyes for about three minutes after the relaxation exercise, then opened them while reporting that she had not been able to visualize herself doing what she desired. She had never dreamed about what she wanted to do in life. Being a good student in math and enjoying teaching had been enough for her. She had a place in her family and had never imagined herself having her own dreams and desires. In short, Anita had never questioned her life.

I was not surprised when I listened to her relay these thoughts. Conditioning is a strong force, and women are often taught to be invisible. Anita had always been busy doing what she was supposed to do according to her family, especially her parents. There had never been space for dreaming a different kind of life or for designing her working life.

As opposed to Anita, my student Leo discovered early in his life that it was really fun to sell things. He started buying groceries in the market and selling them to his friends' mothers at their homes. Later on he decided to quit university and travel to Europe with a friend. He spent two years in various European countries working wherever he could in order to make a living. After those two years he went back to Chile and finished his engineering studies at the university. When he first arrived home, he told his parents that he had had enough time and freedom to dream and envision what he wanted to do. As soon as he finished his university studies he would create a startup business, make his company grow in a couple of years, and become a rich man. And he did so.

Leo had returned to Chile with a purpose. He had decided he would create his own communications company. He understood that he needed to state the objective of finishing his engineering studies and becoming a professional in order to be able to turn into a legitimate entrepreneur with access to the required financial resources. He studied as much as he needed to fulfill his objective, and when he was already an engineer he created his communications company according to his purpose. This company stemmed from his vision, desire, and dream. Leo has lived his adulthood according to his dreams, desires, and purpose.

- What have your dreams and desires been during your life?
- Have you been able to express your purpose in words?
- If the answer to the two former questions is yes, how do you feel?
- If the answer is no, what prevented you from dreaming, desiring, or expressing your purpose?
- If the answer is no, how do you feel?

You can visualize your dreams, and you can feel your desires. Your purpose and objectives must be expressed in words. Once again you find the need to align your body, emotions, feelings, and moods with language.

PEL-MET, Step 4: Checking and Asking

Have you ever been completely absorbed in the activity you are performing? If you have, then you are acquainted with the state of flow. While in flow, you are fully immersed in a feeling of energized focus, full involvement, and enjoyment in what you are doing. The state of flow is a good example of transparency. When you are in flow, you stay in transparency and do not need to perform PEL-MET.

PEL-MET is activated when you become aware of a new sensation in your body. The sensation is like a signal that something must be done in order to recover presence-emotions-language alignment.

In Step 4, ask yourself what is your desire, purpose, or objective in the specific situation you are facing. Irrespective of the scope, you need to retrieve what you are after, whether it is your life purpose or how you want to feel after a certain conversation. This is a linguistic action. You need to think, to use your memory, and to verbalize, in an internal conversation, what it is that you want. After phrasing it internally, distinguish the emotion that grabbed you and name it. After that, ask yourself if this emotion is useful and conducive to fulfilling your purpose (or getting a desirable outcome from the specific situation). The answer can only be yes or no.

Several months after the conversation with Anita that you read at the beginning of this chapter, she had been able to expand her world and focus on what it was she desired in that period of her life. She learned to prioritize, and among the many things she wanted to change she focused on what was most important for her at that time. She discovered that she strongly desired to have peaceful, fun, and connected relationships with her children. She turned this desire into her purpose. As long as Anita's children were growing up and needed her care, relating well to them would be the most important thing in her life.

Anita and her husband had developed a routine of talking about their common issues while riding together to buy the weekly groceries or take their seven-year-old boy to a nice playground. If one or the other got angry, Anita or her husband raised their voice and quarreled. Anita completely forgot that their little boy was listening and becoming a part of their quarrel. After three minutes of discussion she and her husband were shouting and saying nasty things to each other on these excursions.

Anita started practicing PEL-MET in this context. At first her intense emotion made it impossible to become aware of a new physical sensation. Anger usually took over and became her boss. Nevertheless she gradually started to pay attention to her physical sensations precisely in those disagreeable moments. Having verbalized her main purpose helped her. It became a reference for future action. Here is her description of what happened when they were driving to the supermarket:

Her husband was at the wheel. He was shouting. She turned her head around and saw her son sitting in the back seat near the door with his hands crossed, his eyes wide open, and his lips tightly closed together. Anita did not say a word. She turned around and performed PEL-MET.

An: "I can feel how my muscles are narrowing my throat."

After a few seconds Anita paid attention to her breathing rhythm. It felt faster than she would have liked. While her husband was talking, she took a deep breath, which her husband probably thought was a sigh. Anita noticed that she was breathing more calmly. She concentrated for a minute on her breathing until it reached normalcy. During this period she kept silent, both externally and internally. Her husband lowered his voice. Anita's internal conversation went on:

An: "I felt very angry. That was my emotion."

After a short while Anita asked herself,

An: "Is this anger useful for my purpose of having a peaceful, fun, and connected relationship with my son and then with my soon-to-be newborn girl? No, it isn't!"

STEP 4:

a. Identify your dream, purpose, objective, or goal in relation to the present situation.

b. Ask yourself if the emotion(s) named in Step 3 is (are) conducive to fulfilling your dream, purpose, objective, or desired outcome.

PEL-MET Step 5: Call for Action

When transparency is broken, you can either be swayed by events as a passive recipient or a victim, or you can actively participate and drive your life into the path you want to follow. The path can be defined by your life purpose, your desire to end a conversation in a certain way, or any other objective. PEL-MET will help you participate actively in your own life through developing the habit of performing the five steps automatically when the situation calls for it.

You have seen that desires, purpose, and objectives are necessary to become the owner of your life. They allow you to make focused decisions and lay the foundation for becoming a coherent and fulfilled person. Nevertheless, you will not get to start your journey if you only state your purpose or objective, or make a decision, and stop there.

- What is needed after making a decision?

Every decision you make must be followed by action. A decision without action can be considered merely a desire.

PEL-MET VERBAL STEPS

This is why the fifth and last step of PEL-MET is a call for action in order to fulfill your purpose or objective. In this step the method asks you to ask a specific question: "What can I do to change the emotion discovered in Step 3 if it is useless or even opposed to attaining my desired outcome (or purpose or objective)?"

Do you remember the story of Leo that you read in this chapter? Leo decided to go to Europe, but he could have stayed home for whatever reason. He might have been afraid to leave with too little money, or anything else could have happened. Knowing Leo's strong will, he probably would not have stayed home lamenting the poor way life had treated him thus far; he might have changed his decision and acted on it. Some people possess the natural ability to connect very easily their purpose to the actions needed to fulfill it. Others need to learn how to make this connection. **PEL-MET allows you to connect your purpose to your actions through the development of a habit.** Learning to identify a new physical sensation and repeating the actions included in each step in their corresponding sequence creates the habit of aligning your body presence with the emotion that manifested in a physical sensation along with your purpose, objective, or desire.

PEL-MET asks you to ask the above question every time you come to Step 5, and phrase it in the same way each time so that you need not think at all. Only through multiple repetitions of the exact sequence in the prescribed form will you be able to create a new habit.

STEP 5:
a. If the answer to the question in Step 4 is yes, quickly think about what you can possibly do to enhance the emotion you are experiencing.
b. If the answer to the question in Step 4 is no, quickly think about what you can do to change that emotion so that you become open to new possible actions.
c. Choose an action and perform it.

An action can be a body movement such as standing up, a deliberate sentence spoken to the person you are talking with, a dance step, or a breath of fresh air. It can also be a phone call to a family member, your coach, or your lawyer. Your intuition, imagination, and creativity are going to be highly exercised in this last part of the last step of PEL-MET. Do not get discouraged if the actions do not come easily to you. If you practice the step repeatedly you will create an inventory of possible actions that you will be able to retrieve. I have said that repetition is necessary for learning, more so if you are creating a new habit. PEL-MET will move from a method that needs to be practiced into a new habit.

The Five Steps of PEL-MET

Now that you have seen each step in some detail, it can be useful to summarize them. In that way you will be able to observe how the presence-emotions-language alignment is shaped.

PEL-MET is a set of sequential steps. Learning it requires that you repeat the same behavior many times in different situations. Don't worry if at first the process seems slow and you are more self-conscious than you would like to be. Through constant repetition there will come a time when the timing seems adequate and the actions are performed automatically. Repetition allows you to re-create transparency with no effort after a physical sensation makes you interrupt what you are doing in order to perform PEL-MET.

The following page shows a blueprint for exercising PEL-MET.

PEL-MET Blueprint

A method for creating the habit of aligning Presence, Emotions, and Language.

STEP 1:
a. Pay attention to a new physical sensation as soon as it arises.
b. Abruptly cease any activity you are doing.
c. Identify the new sensation without using words.
d. Visualize the new sensation.

STEP 2:
a. Register your normal breathing frequency.[32] (Only once, for use as a reference.)

---

32. This registration is to be used only as a reference in Step 2 of PEL-MET. It is invalid for medical purposes. When calm, resting, and lying down, count the number of times your chest rises in one minute.

b. Focus your attention on your present breathing frequency.
c. Visualize yourself at your normal breathing frequency or follow someone else's breathing rhythm if you consider it calm.
d. Observe the reduction of your breathing frequency until it is normal.
e. Observe your normal rhythm for one or two minutes of conscious breathing.

STEP 3:
a. Identify the emotion (or emotions) that are showing up in your body now.
b. Name it (or each one).

STEP 4:
a. Identify your dream, purpose, objective, or goal in relation to the present situation.
b. Ask yourself if the emotion(s) named in Step 3 is (are) conducive to fulfilling your dream, purpose, objective, or goal.

STEP 5:
a. If the answer to the question in Step 4 is yes, quickly think about what you can possibly do to enhance the emotion you are experiencing.

PEL-MET VERBAL STEPS

   b. If the answer to the question in Step 4 is no, quickly think about what you can do to change that emotion so that you become open to new possible actions.

   c. Choose an action and perform it.

REPEAT, REPEAT, REPEAT!

CHAPTER 11

The Power of Conversations

What Is Special about Human Language?

We are similar to non-human mammals in that we have a body and also emotions. PEL-MET shows how important both of them are in human life. On the other hand, mammals have their own languages. Human language distinguishes human beings from other animals, providing us with an extraordinary capacity to create our reality through it.

Let me explain. Why are you reading this book now?

- When did you discover the existence of this book?
- When did you start reading it?
- What are all the actions that took place in between your discovering the book and starting to read it?

You will find that there were a number of conversations that led you and others to perform different actions. For example, you had at least one conversation before your fingers typed Amazon.com, or you went to a bookstore, or someone left this book at your home. For that to take place you must have used language. It does not matter whether the verbiage was in Spanish, English, or Chinese; the types of actions done by language are all the same. After someone recommended that you might like a book they just read, you must have thought, *I want to read that.* They might have told you where you could find it, and then you made the necessary movements to bring it to you. None of that would have happened without the use of language.[33]

You can see that language is in itself an action that can create new realities. It is the nature of human language that allows you to learn and to keep learning from what you previously learned, and so on and so forth. You are a being who takes actions (including linguistic actions). Those actions can create learning, and the learning can change the being you are. There is a permanent, virtual circle connecting being and acting: the being you are can take certain actions, and the actions you take

---

33. Conversations are sometimes defined as communication between two or more people. In this book, talking to yourself or thinking is also considered a conversation.

can change the being you are. By declaring, "Yes, I do!" when the official or the priest asks you if you accept this woman or man as your spouse, you are making a declaration, which is an act that can change your life forever.

Language gives you the possibility of creating the world you want. It also allows you to observe other people's worlds in a state of openness and empathy. If you decide to become the owner of a company after having been an employee in the corporate world, you must have different kinds of conversations with many people. At first these people and their conversations might seem strange to you, since they talk about different things than those you are used to. These are people who dare to declare huge purposes and goals that you would not have allowed yourself to think about before you made the decision to leave the company where you worked. You will need your imagination to dream about new worlds and wealth that you want to build together with others. You will also need to express these dreams in declarations that drive other creative people to be enthused by the passion of your conversation.

In order to enlarge your world, you must learn to diversify the types of actions you can take through widening your scope of observation of the environment, others, and yourself. You will need to create new observers within you, and to have new kinds of conversations with new people. Your passion has to be felt by those you have conversations with. Your body posture—that is, your presence; the feelings you show; and the language you use to express your purpose must contain your passion. In other words, through language you create a narrative that we shall call "your message." When you declare it passionately, your whole body and your flowing emotions become congruent and aligned. New people will listen to you and believe your words.

As you have already seen, becoming aware of the need for presence-emotions-language alignment is the first step in understanding what a conversation is and the power it can bring. Alignment is a process that can be learned and turned into a habit. This will happen through practice and repetition. PEL-MET is a tool that helps you create the habit of alignment. The power of conversations, then, is always subordinate to alignment between your body presence, your emotional state, and the words that are said and listened to.

Outcomes of Conversations

Some time ago, in the context of a coaching workshop in which I was a student, I observed our leader coaching a man. They had agreed that "client R" would track his emotions in his body. When he was asked, "What are you feeling and where are those feelings located in your body?" R started giving explanations about what he had done, thought, or had become aware of in certain circumstances. Every time this happened, the coach interrupted R and instructed him softly, "Stick to your body. Don't allow your mind to interfere." This situation happened several times.

How could that which was called the mind interfere? Whatever R was doing, it prevented him from concentrating on his body sensations, which was the core of the exercise. If you would have asked R to tell you what he was doing instead of paying attention to his body sensations, R would have ultimately said that he had words "inside his head" that did not allow him to just sit, visualize, and feel. These words did not allow R to connect to the experience he had given his consent to have. Furthermore, they disconnected him from his coach. You could say that he was not really performing the exercise.

I am sure that R did want to connect as much as possible to his coach, and really wanted to experience the exercise itself and its outcomes. Nevertheless the words that came to his mind were beyond his control.

I call these words an "internal conversation." This conversation just happens. You do not decide to have it, and if you are not aware of it, it can become the reality of your life at that moment, excluding you from your voluntary experience and estranging you from establishing relationships with the people you are with. I invite you to ask yourself when the last time was that you remember having an internal conversation. I bet it was not long ago.

- Who were you with?
- If you were alone, what were you saying to yourself?
- If you were not alone, what were you saying to yourself?
- Was it the same dialogue you were having with the rest of the people?

Internal conversations might also be called thoughts. A thought is not a thought until it can be expressed in words. In parallel, a conversation is not a conversation if only words participate in them. Our body posture and gestures, and our feelings and emotions, are part of the conversational experience.

In another exercise between two students, the client said suddenly that she felt her coach seemed nervous and that she had lost confidence in his capacity to help her. The client had not heard the actual word *nervousness*; she had felt it in her coach, and had become completely taken by her internal conversation. Probably she stopped listening to her coach. What possibly triggered her internal conversation was the lack of alignment of the coach's presence, the emotions he expressed, and the words he said. She did not listen to the words the coach said. I can assure you that internally the word *confidence* or *trust* invaded the client completely, not allowing her to listen to the coach. As soon as the internal conversation started, the coach lost his client. From that moment on they stopped having one conversation. Each of them had a separate one with themselves.[34]

I hope you see how convenient it is to become an expert in detecting presence-emotions-language alignment in others and in yourself. While practicing, I suggest you ask yourself if these three gifts are acting in harmony. If they are not, you might be in danger of creating an issue with **trust**. (The topic of trust is covered in chapter 16.) The person you are talking to might believe you are not sincere, or that you lack the needed skills,

---

34. If you are interested in studying the topic of internal and external conversations more deeply, look at the exercise developed by Prof. Donald Schon and Chris Argyris at http://www.fastcompany.com/659549/leading-ideas-surface-your-difficult-issues.

or that you are not capable of delivering what you promised. That person might also think you are too fragile or too tough to handle the situation.

If you know someone does not trust you, and you want to relate to that person, you are responsible for restoring trust or at least creating windows of confidence that will allow you to interact.

- What would you do to regain someone's trust if they told you they no longer have it for you?

It should be easy to see that you have conversations almost all the time during your waking hours, especially if you agree to consider written language, thoughts, and internal conversations as such. I have said that regardless of which language we use, human language is active and it generates new realities.

Last year I travelled as far as Los Angeles, California, from Santiago, Chile, to attend two seminars. I consider that the outcome of those seminars was very fruitful since it provided a vision for my business, which had been confusing and unclear for me prior to attending them. How did I get my new vision? It came simply through conversations with multiple like-minded people I met at the events, and also through my internal conversations and my thoughts. And how did I get to attend the seminars? It all started with conversations in email form, followed by listening to several teleseminars and webinars (all of them conversations). Then I joined two Internet courses in which I created many new relationships through conversations with people belonging to several Facebook and LinkedIn groups. Later on I met many of my new friends in person during the seminars. If I had not received those first anonymous emails, which were not even personal conversations, I might not be writing this book. Those conversations, which were ultimately language and its alignment with my presence and the emotions I felt, determined a new reality for me, including the shaping of my business and the goals and decisions I made for the following year.

This is the power of conversations and human language: no more and no less than the power of shaping your world, creating and maintaining relationships, and getting things done. In your business or at the company where you work, the quality of your conversations determines its feasibility, effectiveness, opportunities, and success or failure.

If you can see that language is action and it creates realities, I have no doubt that you can also see the power of language in human life. That is why I think it is necessary to learn how to converse appropriately so that you create the best possible future for yourself, your colleagues, your clients, and your loved ones.

The Basic Linguistic Actions in Conversations

When you are having a conversation with someone, there are two distinct actions you take:[35]

---

35. Most of what I know about conversations stems from studying a discipline called ontology of language. (See Rafael Echeverría, *Ontología del Lenguaje*, 1994.) I translated the original papers from the first "Mastering the Art of Pro-

- You listen.
- You speak.

If you are having a conversation with yourself, you also perform these two actions. It might be fun to gain awareness that you are in the midst of an internal conversation and distinguish whether you are listening or speaking. Observe how different these two modalities of language are and how they dance with each other.

You could take a third action, which is to remain silent. Silence can have the same effect in a conversation that it has in music: it can be a welcome pause. And the proper use of silence can be highly responsible for the good quality of a conversation, just as in music.

Nevertheless, silence can also be used as an expression of feelings that promote disconnection between the participants in a conversation. You do not choose what emotions to have, but you can certainly choose to create an emotional difficulty for the person or the group you are interacting with at any given time.

In that context, silence is the consequence of a decision in which you want to demonstrate something by using it. Have you ever had the experience of children who do not talk to each other when they are angry? Or a wife who does not speak to her husband in order to show him that he did something wrong? Or a daughter who does not speak to a parent, or vice

---

fessional Coaching" course given by Rafael Echeverría and Julio Olalla from English into Spanish in 1991. These translations, with several addendums, are the basis of the book in reference. Olalla and Echeverría had worked on the topic of ontological design with Fernando Flores et al. in California, USA.

versa? At work, when the employees are not satisfied or they live in fear, they usually create a routine consisting of silent behavior. Sometimes this silent routine can become a boycott or a style of protest.

In order to overcome the effects of this type of silence and also break it, strong leadership capabilities are needed. A prolonged, deliberate silence can be harmful to a couple's future together, to family life, or to the organizational health of a company.

- Choose an example of deliberate silence experienced by you.
- What were the consequences?
- Would it have been desirable to break the silence?
- Why? Name one or more benefits that breaking the silence would have brought.
- What would you have done in order to break the silence?

In several of the chapters that follow you will have the opportunity to observe the power of these distinctions as tools for self-development, establishing and maintaining relationships, and developing sustainable leadership at work and in any other field you choose to engage in.

CHAPTER 12

The Magic of Listening

Solving the Mystery of Listening

Have you ever heard the idea that listening corresponds to the reception of a message produced by a source that emits it and then is transferred to the human ear? This would mean that I speak (issuer), and my words are transmitted by some means, and then you hear or listen (receiver). The environment might interfere, producing certain "noises" that can be corrected. My mouth is the transmitter, the signal is the sound waves, and your ear is the receiver. "Noise" includes any distraction you might experience as I speak.

This is an existing human communication model. It assumes that what is said is what is listened to. In this model, speaking and listening are part of the same, single process. It assumes that you, as the receiver, listen passively to what I say. It is known as Weaver and Shannon's communication model, developed in 1949 by these two engineers.[36] Shannon wrote a two-page paper in 1948 in the context of developing a mathematical model for communication of information at Bell Labs in New Jersey, USA, and Weaver transformed the content into a model that could be understood by everyone. It was not only adopted by communication and information engineers, but it is still being used, to this day, to describe human communication.

Unfortunately the widespread use of this model might be an important factor in poor communication among human beings. It was conceived for the transfer of information to machines and things, not to living organisms. Human communication is altogether different.

To begin with, listening is not a passive part of speaking. The action of speaking and the action of listening are two separate processes that run their own ways. They are both active and different: the person who speaks decides to do so, whereas **listening happens.**

Listening is not hearing. The latter is a biological input for a brain process that results in listening. Your ear hears and sends a signal to your brain, which combines several factors resulting in your listening.

---

36. http://www.oxfordreference.com/view/10.1093/oi/authority.20110803100459436

The person who speaks says what they want to say. The one who listens does not necessarily listen to what is being said, but to a combination of their hearing plus processing in their mind according to several factors.

Speaking does not ensure listening!

You can see that speaking is an act of will, although we sometimes say out loud something we later regret. Emotions and biology never leave us!

On the contrary, hearing is not a voluntary act. There is a noise or sound that stimulates your ear. That information travels to your brain where it encounters your mood, intentions, inner conversations, early conditioning, and mindset. Through this process you give meaning to what you hear. This complex process is what we are naming *listening* in this book.

The absence of awareness of the fact that a conversation consists of two different phenomena, listening and speaking, creates many of the present communication problems in every field of human relationship and activity.

I have asked dozens of people to tell me what a conversation is in their own terms. The general answer is, "We are having a conversation when we are speaking to someone." Seldom do people include listening in the definition. Most of us have internalized the one-process model in which listening is the outcome of speaking.

- How would you define a conversation?

I was Anton's coach for some months. He did not come to me on his own accord, but was sent by the human resources manager[37] of the company where they both worked. He was the sales manager of the company and could not realize, and less so acknowledge, that several of his collaborators feared and resented him. In turn, he was resentful of every person in the organization who might have expressed a negative comment about his management and leadership style.

Anton told me that he was perplexed. He knew very few people who were as clear and transparent in giving instructions and feedback as he was. Except for two or three people who had complained about his style, and Anton was sure they had obscure reasons for doing so, his yearly performance assessments had been consistently good throughout the years he had held this position in the company.

I listened to him speak for a long time. When he came to a stop, I asked, "Anton, do you usually check with your team to see if they really listened to what you said to them?"

Anton looked surprised and replied, "Why would I do that? Isn't it inappropriate to ask adult people if they understand me? Believe me, there's no way that somebody could misunderstand my words. I know how clear I am!"

Anton clearly adhered to the one-process model of communication even though he was unaware of doing so. This

---

37. I suggest creating a movement to change the use of the terms *human resources* and *human capital* to *people development* and *collaboration*.

was his way of thinking. It was embedded in his mindset, and he was perfectly blind to the fact that listening is much more complex than just hearing a message.

Listening is an active process. You are not merely a passive recipient of what is said. You listen according to who you are: your history, your culture, and your conditioning. The various observers within you generate different listenings to the same words. You are a better listener if what is said is of interest to you. You will not get rid of your own expectations, assumptions, and mood. They taint your listening. When you trust the speaker, you listen better than when you do not. Sensing presence-emotions-language alignment in the speaker creates trust. In the preceding chapter there was an example of an internal conversation being triggered as soon as someone lost their trust in the speaker. From that moment on they do not listen to the other person at all because they are busy listening only to their internal conversation about mistrust, or formulating a preconceived comment.

In Anton's case, skipping the complexity of listening has brought him relationship difficulties that he cannot even begin to deal with since he does not concede the benefit of a doubt upon his knowledge and beliefs.

I invite you to open up to a different way of observing the dance between speaking and listening.

- What is your ultimate purpose when you speak?

When I speak, I do so because I want one or more people to listen to me. Without listeners, there are no speakers. In other words, I will not speak if there is no one to listen to me.

If I speak because I want someone to listen, then listening is more important than speaking, for the consequences of listening are the ones that will produce new events, and not the speaking itself.

Listening validates speaking.

When you speak, you are accountable to a great extent for the quality of listening of the people to whom you are speaking. You must create trust, interest, and even new possibilities for them. That will keep them focused on what you are saying and they will open up to the experience of listening.

If you have ever read stories to a small child, you will be able to grasp this concept as part of your experience. If you want the child to sleep, you will not concentrate on their listening; on the contrary, you want them to stop paying attention to your reading and go to sleep. But if you are reading while playing with the child, you will have to do a lot more than read in a monotone voice in order to have them listen to the story. You will need to draw the child's attention to the story by dramatizing and creating emotions in them.

How You Can Improve Your Listening

Attention, one of the three gifts I called the Three Graces, is one of the tools you can use to improve your listening. Although listening happens automatically, you can improve it if you learn when and how to pay more attention than your usual unconscious standard when needed. If PEL-MET becomes a habit, you will pay attention when you want to ensure good listening habits.

Here are three more actions I suggest you take in order to become an even better listener:

1. If you are the listener, verify with the speaker that what you listened to corresponds to what they said. If you are the speaker, verify that what you said is precisely what was listened to.

   - How would you check if someone listened effectively to what you said?
   - What would you do to check if you listened well to what was said?

2. Allow your partner in the conversation to express their concerns regardless of whether you are the listener or the speaker. If you are the speaker you will need to verify whether or not what was listened to is what you said. If

you are the listener, check that you are really interested in listening and not just waiting for your turn to reply.[38]

Below you will see two different ways to conduct a conversation between Roberta and her daughter, Connie, who is a student on summer holiday. They are in the hallway near the entrance of their home. Connie is getting ready to leave the house.

Conversation 1:
R: "Are you going out, Connie?"
C: "Yes, Mom. I'm late."
R: "How much money are you taking with you?"
C: "I don't know . . . let me check."

Connie looks for her purse, counts her money, and says,

C: "I am taking $500, which I received as payment for the month I spent working at the library."

Roberta says, raising her voice,

R: "Leave the money here!"
C: "No, I will not!"

---

[38]. In the fifth habit of Stephen Covey's book *The 7 Habits of Highly Effective People* (Simon and Schuster, 2013), which he named "Seek First to Understand; Then to be Understood," he writes a critical assessment of our listening habits: "Most people do not listen with the intent to understand; they listen with the intent to reply."

R: "I am telling you ... leave the money at home!"
C: "Don't yell at me!"
R: "You're the one that's yelling!"
C: "I don't want to hear any more!"

Connie puts back her purse in her bag and while she is doing that, leaves the house, slamming the door.

Conversation 2:
R: "Are you going out, Connie?"
C: "Yes, Mom. I'm late."
R: "Connie, just give me a second. Are you taking money with you?"
C: "Yes, why? Let me look."

While Connie is searching for her purse in the bag, Roberta says,

R: "Because I was robbed yesterday. I didn't have the opportunity to tell you until now."
C: "Wow! How did it happen?"
R: "I will tell you some other time, Dear, since you are late. Just be careful to take only the money you need and not to wear any jewelry. I am very scared."
C: "Of course, Mom. I'm sorry I cannot stay now, but I'll do my best to come home early. Can you take this money to my room? I earned it at the library this month."

R: "Sure. Please take good care of yourself and come home early."
C: "Don't worry, Mom. Bye."

- Which conversation would you have liked better?
- What are the reasons for your preference?

3. Inquire, that is, ask questions, or get clarification if you still have not found the equivalent between what was said and what was listened to.

- Recall a conversation that could have ended better if you had asked some questions for clarification.

Have you ever had a misunderstanding with someone? If so, it probably happened because of the inevitable gap between speaking and listening. You are always responsible for what you say. Nevertheless, if you are the listener and you feel or think you did not grasp what was said, it is your responsibility to pay attention, check if you really listened to what was said, clarify what drove your partner to the conversation, and share the speaker's concerns with yours. You can ask for all possible clarification that will lead you to bridge the gap between what was said and what was received.

Probably the late Stephen R. Covey would have asked you to listen in order to listen, and not to listen in order to reply. If you concentrate on your reply instead of on listening, you will have an internal conversation that can prevent you even from hearing what the other person is saying.

- I invite you to remember two conversations that ended in a misunderstandings. In one of them you were the speaker and in the other you were the listener. Think them over and discover what would have happened if both the listener and the speaker were attentive and used the other three tips I suggested above.

Opportunities that Listening Provides: Understanding and Transformation

Listening allows you to open up to understanding another person if you do so with respect, accepting them as legitimate in their diversity and autonomy from yourself. If they are your partner in a conversation, you acknowledge your different interpretations of the world around you that determine different actions in their life than in your own. Listening with respect to a new interpretation can open new spaces of action that you might not even have imagined.

This is the kind of listening that you must practice in negotiations. Each party needs to understand the other's concerns in order to be willing to find common ground that will make it easier for each of them to make concessions.

If you listen with openness to diversity, attention, and trust, you might have the opportunity to be transformed. Let me give you a personal example:

In 1983, I had the opportunity to translate, at the time of the seminar, and later in written form, a seminar given in Chile by the late Vimala Thakar,[39] a spiritual guide who had been a disciple of Jiddu Krishnamurti.[40] Many people, myself included, agree that whatever Thakar said was so powerful that it could always be quoted. I will address only one of the several things she said that transformed me from a troubled, lonely soul to a peaceful and connected one, just by listening attentively to her charismatic words.

Thakar said:

"For me, religion and spirituality is one and the same. Religion does not refer to institutions like Hinduism, Christianism, Buddism, Islamism, or any other 'ism.' These institutions are wrongly called religion. They are lifestyles, ways of living. They have authorities, books, and are related to specific communities. Religion and spirituality are consciously united with the totality of existence, with the totality of universal life. There cannot be more than one religion, that of communion with the known, the unknown and the unknowable of the totality of the universe, with which all beings are connected."

---

39. You can learn more about Vimala Thakar at http://www.servicespace.org/blog/view.php?id=2038.
40. If you want to know more about Jiddu Krishnamurti, go to http://www.jkrishnamurti.org.

My sense of relief was indescribably strong when I listened to Thakar say that there is no more than one religion. I spent some days in a different frequency, feeling that I was deeply connected to the people gathered there, to the food we ate, and to the trees and the birds and the dogs. I had never had an experience like this one before. For the first time in my life I felt a deep connection and a sense of belonging to this universe, in communion with all its beings.

> - Can you remember being a listener in a conversation that transformed who you were? Recall it in detail.

One of the most important features of a leader is their capacity to listen to their stakeholders and their team. It is through listening that you can obtain most of the information needed to determine what your team needs to learn and what it needs to improve. Having conversations with your team and listening actively to what they tell you contribute importantly to your success as a leader.

Listening is just as important in organizations as it is at home. Couples who expand their understanding and are transformed by their conversations with their spouses, and parents who learn to listen to their children more than they talk to them, even before the latter can interact through language, experience fulfillment.

CHAPTER 13

Creating New Realities through the Act of Speaking

Two Modalities of Speaking: Proposal and Inquiry

You have already seen that listening and speaking are two very different types of actions that take place during a conversation. Listening is involuntary; it is affected by many circumstances, and you have a certain responsibility for the quality of your listening. It is better to pay respectful attention and use the available tools for clarity by checking what was said, sharing concerns, and inquiring about what it is that made the speaker say what they said.

Speaking is not an action that occurs to you like listening. If you speak, it is because you have made a decision to do so. In that sense, all the actions that you do while you speak are your choice and your responsibility. If you look at the relationship between the listener and speaker, the latter is responsible for how they are going to be listened to. It is easier to think that the listener will pay attention if they feel respected by the speaker. Sometimes, due to cultural differences or the speaker's ignorance about the listener's history, emotions, and conditioning, the speaker can say something that the listener feels is an invalidation of their being, or as disrespectful, whereas the speaker had no intention of causing that feeling in the listener. This implies that the speaker should also use all the tools for a good listener.

- When do you speak?

This question has already been answered when we discussed the action of listening. Nevertheless I invite you to answer it again while placing yourself now in the role of the speaker.

What has already been said is that you speak in order to be listened to because there is something you want someone to know or to do. Without a listener, speaking becomes senseless.

That is one reason for speaking: you propose an observation or an interpretation, including the course of action that seems best for you. You speak in order to be listened to and create future action in your listener.

For example, the leader of a corporate team says, "The marketing manager handed me the sales goals that our company has decided we must meet this quarter. I find them challenging, so I have the following proposal to make to all of you."

There is yet another reason for speaking: you speak in order to listen. You want to know what the concerns of the listener are, so you ask (inquire) in order for them to speak. Questions are typical examples of this form of speaking. You speak while you ask a question, and what you are interested in is listening to the answer you will receive.

Let us continue with the example we started above. After making his proposal, the team leader remained quiet for a while and then asked, "Is there someone who wants to contribute with an idea that could help us meet our goals in an even better way?" This time the team leader spoke in order to listen to other people, not to be listened to.

Although questions are the general form of inquiry, you do not necessarily need to inquire by means of a question. Suppose your client Fred just told you something about himself. You listened carefully, but did not understand clearly. You can say, "Tell me more about it, Fred." There is no question here, and yet you are inquiring; you are speaking to let the other person speak.

- Recall the last proposal you made. Was it accepted? Was it carried out? What do you think are the reasons for its success or failure?
- Recall the last inquiry you made. Did you obtain the information you needed? Could you have said something else to obtain a better result?
- What is the proportion of proposals to inquiries that you usually make? How can you interpret what that proportion might indicate about you?

In certain cultures people tend to propose more than inquire, and vice-versa. When you propose, you are basically concerned about things going your way. When you inquire, you open up to the possibility of understanding something or someone better and to be transformed. It is beneficial to find a balance between the modalities in your daily life. Practicing the act of inquiring allows you to feel receptive to new ideas and empowered to make proposals that will be well-considered by others.

The Acts of Speech: Are You Describing or Creating Your World?

We have seen that language is action and it creates reality. This can be observed very clearly when you distinguish the actions involved and the different responsibilities that each speech act demands from the speaker.

CREATING NEW REALITIES THROUGH THE ACT OF SPEAKING

Let us begin by looking at the acts of speech from the perspective of the ontology of language.[41]

When you observe speech as an action, you are necessarily establishing a link between the word and the world. A very important question that stems from this observation is what has the lead in the conversation? Is it the word or the world? Which leads to action?

Sometimes it is the world that leads the word to action, and sometimes the word demands an adjustment of your world. This allows you to distinguish two very different speech acts: assertions and declarations.[42]

> ASSERTIONS: When you make an assertion, the word adapts to the world. You observe and say what the world shows you. You describe what you see.

Right now I am drinking a glass of water. In the Western world, everyone will agree that what I am holding is a glass, and that it contains a clear liquid, which I am drinking. When I say it, those elements are already in the world. My words have followed the world. "I am drinking a glass of water" is an assertion in which I describe what I am doing in this world now.

> DECLARATIONS: When you make a declaration, the world must adapt to the word. The word has the power to modify the world.

---

41. See Reference 35, chapter 11: The ontology of language finds its source in the works of J. L. Austin; J. Searle; L. Wittgenstein; H. Maturana; F. Flores, and others.
42. Ibid.

Last week my friend Ruby said to a couple who had moved into her apartment, "Enough is enough. I want you out!" These two sentences will create a very different world for both Ruby and her couple. She made a declaration. Their world will have to adapt to her words.

I invite you now to go a little bit deeper in your understanding of assertions and declarations. My goal is that after reading this section you will be prepared to distinguish between them in your daily life without confusing one with the other. Both speech acts demand different responsibilities. If you confuse them, you will create a communication problem. Listening will become difficult and you will soon experience the emergence of misunderstanding.

We shall start with the speech act assertion.

When you look at something outside of yourself, like an accounting balance sheet, a glass, clothes, an object, or data from a report, you can share it with others and there will be a common understanding about what you are referring to. Your society, or the community in which you live, has decided to name the same objects with the same words. As already said, the word must adapt to the world. You do not invent names for common objects; they are out there in the world. Your responsibility is to say the truth. If you make an observation and someone does not believe you, you need to provide the evidence that what you are saying is true. The evidence consists of one or more facts that show the truth of what you are saying. Evidence must be factual, not merely one's interpretation of the event.

CREATING NEW REALITIES THROUGH THE ACT OF SPEAKING

Many years ago I watched a film that took place in Africa during the eighties. The characters belonged to the Maasai people, who live very simple lives in eastern Africa and are known for their peaceful and relaxed coexistence. At that time their lifestyle was very different from that of the Western world. The film told the story of the many changes that this community suffered after an event took place in their area. Someone who was flying a helicopter threw an object out of the window, which eventually hit a young man on the head. The village gathered around the young man and made all kinds of hypotheses and interpretations about what the object was, since it did not belong to the Maasais' world. This gave birth to arguments, quarrels, divisions, and a new behavior. Their peaceful life was completely disrupted and they started fighting each other.

In this case the word took precedence over the world, and they needed to adjust it. They had to make sense of that object which had fallen from the sky. They would not recover their peaceful coexistence until they decided collectively on a name, description, and meaning for the object. For some, the meaning was a divine call from heaven; for others it was an object with no meaning. Others thought it was a revelation of something sacred. One thing was common: All the different groups wanted to retain the object, so for the first time for the Maasai, power struggles began.

The people seeing the film in the Western world recognized the object with no trouble at all. No matter who you would have asked what the object was, they would have made the assertion "It is an empty Coca-Cola bottle." They could also have provided evidence for that assertion by saying, "See? The logo is engraved on it." So for a huge number of people in the world, the empty bottle itself would have provided the evidence of what it was. This is a true assertion for many people, but for the Maasai the true assertion was "This is an unidentified object that fell from the sky and bumped into a man's head."

A true assertion does not awaken controversy. Controversies come up when people think differently and do not accept the legitimacy of diversity. For them the world is a binary entity in which you can have truth (their truth) or falsehood (whatever deviates from their truth). They live as owners of truth and do not distinguish between assertions and declarations. They go through life as if the world is a fixed thing and the only thing someone else can do about it is describe its content, provided the description coincides with theirs. For them, language does not create reality. The reality is there and it is the one they observe.

These people do not realize that thoughts cannot be true or false. You create your thoughts, often in consideration of influences received from your environment. You might remember, from previous chapters, that all humans are the same in terms of species; similar to others; and at the same time unique. That uniqueness, which I have called your soul, is what allows you to create your thoughts and to create new worlds in language. The possible new worlds are the outcome of saying a declaration, not an assertion.

Lorna and Alfred are the parents of Ruth, a sixteen-year-old girl. While they are having dinner the telephone rings, and Ruth is the first to get to the phone. Both Lorna and Alfred look at their watches and continue eating. After ten minutes, Alfred raises his voice, saying, "That's enough, Ruth! Come back and finish your dinner." Five minutes later Ruth comes back to the table and continues eating. "Who was that?" asks Alfred after some moments of silence. "No one," replies Ruth.

- Finish the story using your imagination.
- Is "no one" an assertion?
- If it is, is it true or false? Does it require evidence?[43]

Assume you have received a report at your office. The numbers surprise you because you cannot understand the variations from the last report. What would you do in that case? I would certainly verify the numbers in the last report and in the new one. If you find something wrong with the numbers, you will know that you have been provided false assertions. If you had not asked for evidence of the correctness of the numbers, you would not have discovered that you were given false information.

Assertions are the information that connects us to the outside world. If you can provide evidence of your assertion, it will be a true one. If the evidence that is provided does not allow you to arrive at the given information, you are either facing a false assertion or you need more evidence than that provided. If you cannot find it, you might need some more bookkeeping

---

43. In this case, Ruth's answer, "No one," is a self-evident false assertion. It does not require evidence, but probably it does require a tranquil parent-daughter conversation.

and statistics. You might also require modifications or the introduction of new procedures that will allow you to find that kind of evidence systematically.

Now let's go back in time to May 25th of 1961, a special day for the world and for the United States in particular. In the midst of the cold war and the space race between the Soviet Union and the United States, on May 25th President John F. Kennedy gave a "Special Message to Congress on Urgent National Needs." He said that those were extraordinary times and that the country was facing an extraordinary challenge "to take a clearly leading role in space achievements, which in many ways may hold the key to our future on earth."[44] The president said that not enough resources were being spent for the purpose of world space leadership, and that is why he asked the members of Congress to approve the required funds needed to achieve the goal of landing a man on the moon and returning him safely to earth before the turn of the decade.

Kennedy was assassinated on November 22nd, 1963, while on an official visit to Dallas. He died a little more than two years after his special speech to Congress and did not have the opportunity to see his fellow countrymen landing and walking on the moon before the end of the decade.

As sad as this may be, we can assert as a fact that after Kennedy's speech to Congress many things started to happen at NASA: mainly conversations that allowed this institution to fulfill his dream. On July 20th, 1969, Apollo 11's lunar module Eagle landed on the moon in the Sea of Tranquility, with astronauts

---
44. http://www.azquotes.com/quote/909882

CREATING NEW REALITIES THROUGH THE ACT OF SPEAKING

Neil Armstrong and Buzz Aldrin aboard. A dozen men would walk on the moon before the Apollo program ended in 1975. The development of medical technologies, weather forecasting, computer technology, and telecommunications can all trace their origins to the space program.[45]

- What did Kennedy do?

Kennedy made a declaration.[46] This declaration gave birth to hundreds of thousands of conversations (actions) among a huge number of people. They made it possible, for the sake of humanity, to fulfill the dream of one man who had the authority to proclaim it and change the world. His word preceded the world. Had he not made the declaration, our world would not be the same today.

If you are married, what happened to your world when the priest, rabbi, or civil official said, "I now declare you husband and wife"? And when you were told "I love you" for the first time, what impact did it have in your world? Do you remember what happened when your parents said, "No!" after you asked them for permission to go somewhere?

In all these cases, just as in the adventure of going to the moon, the word has the power to change the world in some form or other. The word comes from within the person who says it. Unlike assertions, declarations are not true or false. Your responsibility in making a declaration is not to provide

---

45. NASA: www.nasa.gov
46. You can see a video with an 8- minute excerpt of Kennedy's speech at: http://www.jfklibrary.org/Asset-Viewer/xzw1gaeeTES6khED14P1Iw.aspx

evidence; it is to have the authority to make it. Do you have the authority to declare a couple man and wife? Do you have the authority to tell your son that you love him? We need to be given the authority to make certain declarations. If I manage to go to Congress and speak very eloquently about my dream of a leadership paradigm shift that will improve the well-being of all the citizens of the planet, without having been given the authority by other authorities, my declaration might be nice to hear, but it would not be valid. If I write the same declaration in this book, I do have the authority to write it because I am the author of this book.

Having the authority to make a declaration is your first responsibility, yet it is not the only one. Without the hundreds of thousands of conversations that took place between 1961 and 1969, mankind might not have reached the moon in 1969 regardless of how inspiring Kennedy's declaration had been. If the man you love says, "I want to marry you," he has the authority to say it and also the responsibility to do things like requesting, offering, promising, making more declarations, and evaluating, together with you, such issues as which is the best moment and place to get married. Everybody has the authority to make this declaration, but not everyone realizes that after making it they become responsible for a lot of activities that must be performed, mostly linguistic activities. Those activities lead to specific actions that allow the declaration to become reality.

A declaration is valid or invalid, not true or false like an assertion. In order for it to be valid, the person who makes the declaration must have the authority to do so. They must also

CREATING NEW REALITIES THROUGH THE ACT OF SPEAKING

create the conditions, through a series of linguistic actions, for the spoken words to become a reality. As already seen, you have the authority to say, "I want to marry you," but that alone does not make your declaration valid. You must perform many linguistic actions to make your wedding a reality. Only then is it possible to say that your declaration was a valid one.

Declarations can create or modify worlds. Just consider which worlds are closed and opened when someone says yes, no, thanks, I love you, I hate you, enough is enough, stop, goal! (in soccer), or even please forgive me!

- Write down all the declarations you can think of.
- Who has the authority to make each one?
- What are the actions that will need to be taken in order for the declaration to become a reality?

Now let's turn to your experience with declarations. The following exercise will show you how powerful declarations are. Take notice of the difference between declarations and assertions from an experiential point of view.

- What is the last declaration you made and what happened afterward?
- Where in your body did you feel the declaration?
- What emotions did it produce?
- What is (are) the declaration(s) you would like to make, yet have not?
- What is preventing you from making it (them)?

If we go back to the need to align presence, emotions, and language, you might find a flavor of PEL-MET in the last exercise because there is an inevitable link between what you feel and what you say. Your feelings and emotions predispose you to use language in a certain way and thus make certain declarations and not others.

Your awareness of emotional intensity helps you clarify and dare to make the declarations you need to make. And the way I propose to explore your emotions in order to discover what linguistic actions are possible and not possible for you starts with addressing your body sensations.

Observing your presence and your emotions gives you important reasons to practice PEL-MET in your daily life. Turn it into a habit, and you will be able to make powerful, transformational declarations that can affect your life and the lives of others you care about. This is one way to transform your world and build a heart-centered path for fulfillment.

CHAPTER 14

A Special Kind of Declaration

Declarations That Judge

There is one type of declaration whose consequences and conditions of validation go beyond the ones we have already seen. For that reason it is considered a speech act in its own right. We call it an assessment.

Assessments are comprised of judgment, evaluation, appraisal, estimation, interpretation, qualification, and opinion. They are so widely used that some people call humans "assessment-making machines."

Would you say that the following sentence is an assertion?: "She is twenty-three years old."

Yes, it is, and you can find the evidence by looking at her identification. If she was born twenty-three years before today, this is a true assertion.

Now look at the sentence: "She is young." Is this also an assertion?

In spite of having the same grammatical form, "X is Y," the two sentences correspond to different speech acts. In the first one, the world precedes the word. The assertion is true or false depending on the evidence provided. The validity of the second one depends on whether the speaker thinks twenty-three is young according to their beliefs and thoughts. The word precedes the world, as in any declaration. "She is young" is not an assertion; it is an assessment. It is not true or false, but rather valid or invalid, as is any declaration. (You will read more about validation of assessments later in this chapter.)

Suppose Yvonne, six-year-old Damian's mother, is the person who made this assessment about her son's teacher after meeting her for the first time. Naturally Yvonne does not know the teacher's exact age.

- What would probably be Damian's assessment?

Let me give you my prediction. I think Damian would probably argue with his mother that the teacher is not young since all teachers are old to a young child. If I listened to this assessment I would be able to know something about Damian even without seeing him. I would surely say that we are talking about a little boy.

A SPECIAL KIND OF DECLARATION

Notice how powerful an assessment can be! Not only does it make an evaluation or interpretation about someone or something, it can also say a lot about the person who is making the assessment. This can get really tricky when the assessment has a moral or value content, or when it hides negative feelings. You hear what someone is saying about someone's way of being or their behavior, and at the same time you listen to what the assessor did not say but that portrays their way of being or their feelings.

Here is an example:

Lola and Nicole are classmates in college. They have been together since their first year in primary school, and their teachers and peers consider them to be quite beautiful and intelligent. Nicole has always had slightly better grades than Lola. Lola has a boyfriend, and Nicole does not. Last Friday they had the following conversation:

N: "Lola, do you have a minute? I need to tell you something."
L: "Of course. I'm curious. Tell me."
N: "As of yesterday evening, Tommy is my boyfriend."
L: "No! Really? How did it happen?"
N: "It just happened. We both saw it coming."
L: "Hmm . . . be careful. It might not work. I don't think you can keep your good grades if you use your study time to be with Tommy."

- Is there an assessment in the conversation?
- If there is, what is it? Formulate it in your own words.
- Who made it?
- What can you say about the person who made the assessment?

Assessments make sense of the facts of life. They color them with nuance and provide the world with richness of diversity. They show us that we can learn and make the world a better place. And they can destroy the image and the life of a person when those who make them do not take responsibility for their validation.

Assessments and Time

Assessments are time sensitive; assertions are not. A glass is a glass today, tomorrow, and also in the past. You might consider the teacher young today and in the past; but in the future she will no longer be young.

When you make an assessment, you make a verdict in the present. Your assessment shows what you think the future of the topic will look like, whether you are conscious of that or not. And you also look for facts you have observed in the past that allow you to make the verdict today (see Figure 1).

A SPECIAL KIND OF DECLARATION

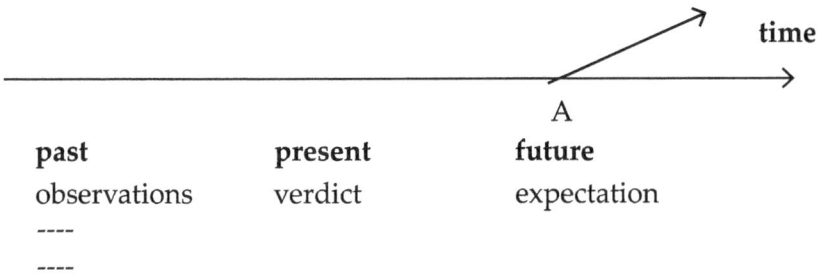

Figure 1

If the observed facts do not change, it is probable that in the future you will make the same assessment, following a straight line from past to present to future. But if the facts are no longer the same and, for example, Brenda changes her behavior at point A in time (see Figure 1), some of the observations about Brenda made in the past will not be made now. Therefore you cannot expect the future to be the same as the present and past. The timeline will change its course concerning your new expectations for the future, and you will make a different assessment.

The possibility of changing an assessment is one of the distinctions between an assertion and an assessment.

Let's zoom in on Brenda's story.

She is a vivacious young woman in her thirties working as a marketing agent in an important international company in New York. Brenda had been late to meet a client for the last three scheduled appointments. Today she was late for the team meeting with her boss, Martin. They waited five minutes, then

Martin started the meeting. Everybody could see that he was angry and frustrated. Brenda arrived fifteen minutes later, so she missed almost half the meeting. Martin's mood did not improve throughout the rest of the day.

When Martin and Tina, his wife, were having dinner, she asked him:

T: "Is something bothering you, Martin?"

After a few seconds of hesitation, he answered,

M: "You know something, Tina? Actually, there is something bothering me. It has been bothering me the whole day, and I haven't been able to get rid of it."

He seemed hesitant again.

T: "Well, are you going to tell me what's going on?"

Martin sighed and started speaking monotonously:

M: "Have I told you about this girl, Brenda, who is part of my team?"
T: "I think I've heard that name. Yes, I remember. You seemed to like her."
M: "She has very good ideas. And she gets along smoothly with the rest of the team. Nevertheless, I cannot trust her."
T: "Why? She seems good at her job."
M: "But she is unpunctual. I've counted at least three instances

in which she was late for a meeting with a client. Just imagine! What if one day a client complains or gets angry and leaves us?"

There was silence for thirty seconds or so, and then Tina asked,

T: "Has anybody talked to her about this?"
M: "If anybody should do so it would have to be me. But why would I talk to her? Being on time is a basic requirement for any employee."
T: "Martin, Dear, would I have understood what was happening to you if I hadn't asked you?"
M: "Hmm... not likely. I will talk to Brenda tomorrow morning."

Martin and Brenda did have a conversation. She told him that she was going through a tough time because she had recently divorced her husband and their four-year-old boy suffered from chronic obstructive bronchitis. This required her to take him to the hospital for his treatment when he had an episode, which happened quite frequently in the wintertime. Brenda assured Martin that everything was under control and that she had informed those three clients who had to wait for her that she could be late because of this. She had called all three of them at least ninety minutes before their scheduled appointment. On the other hand, she had not thought it was necessary to inform Martin about her situation before the team meeting because she knew she could count on the help of her colleagues. Brenda promised Martin to arrive on time or else to take all the corresponding measures from that moment on, including informing him beforehand of any delays on her behalf. Martin believed her, and the issue of trust vanished.

From then on Brenda was very careful to let Martin, her clients, and several other people at the office know in advance when she would be late.

I suggest you look at Figure 1 above while we observe what happened:

1. Martin observed four instances when Brenda was late. (four assertions)
2. Martin made a verdict in the present, while having dinner with his wife, Tina. "Brenda is unpunctual." (assessment)
3. Somewhat later, at point A in Figure 1, Martin summoned Brenda to talk about the concerns that his assessment generated. Brenda promised to change some of her behaviors.
4. From point A onward, Brenda fulfilled her promise so that everybody who needed to know she would be late was informed in advance.
5. For Martin, the timeline changed at point A. He would have to make his observations from that point onward to be able to predict Brenda's punctuality in the future.
6. Brenda's new behavior invalidated Martin's previous assessment. She is no longer unpunctual in the eyes of her boss and colleagues.

A SPECIAL KIND OF DECLARATION

When Martin hired Brenda, he also hired Niels, whom he had met when he was a client of the firm where Niels worked. Niels was well known among marketing and advertising firms as an excellent salesman. Martin agreed with this assessment.

In order to accept Martin's offer, Niels asked for a significantly higher salary than the one he was receiving from the other company. Since Martin had high expectations of Niels's performance, he accepted his conditions for employment. He even thought of promoting him, in due time, to the position of marketing manager.

Things did not happen as Martin had planned. He did not only need a good salesman, which Niels was, but he also needed someone with leadership skills to create effective teamwork and distribute and supervise paperwork for a group of collaborators. He required someone with skills in stress management, both for him and for the members of his team. Within six months, Niels was out of the company.

What happened?

Martin had observed Niels's selling skills in the past. On the basis of those skills he made a judgment in the present (when he hired him) that exceeded the scope of that observation. Martin projected Niels's selling skills to other types of skillsets that would be needed, but had not been observed. As it turned out, Niels made fabulous sales but was unable to create a team and supervise paperwork. He was used to working alone and fulfilling demanding sales goals. In a team environment he suffered from such stress that ultimately he was unable to cope with it, and his work performance became unacceptable in regard to Martin's standards.

- What lessons can you learn from this story?

Validation of Assessments

As with any declaration, you need authority or permission to make an assessment. This is the first condition of validation.

Have you ever heard someone say to another person, "Wow, you are so fat!"? If you have said something like this before, be aware that you might not have been given permission to make such an assessment, nor to say it out loud. The people listening to you probably considered you disrespectful, especially the supposedly fat person. At any rate, they must have been concerned about their weight and the way they looked before you met them. It is not unlikely that their weight is a big and difficult challenge for them. Your assessment will "add salt to the wound," so to speak. Please take care that you have the authority to pass judgment, and pay attention to assessments others make that you will not allow. How often have you suffered in silence because of an assessment made to you that you considered out of place, but did not refute the authority of the person making it? There is no need to suffer rude behavior. Just know that the assessment is invalid, and do not consider it. You can tell the person who made it that you are not allowing that to be said in front of you.

A SPECIAL KIND OF DECLARATION

- Do you remember an assessment that you did not like that was made to you?
- Did you feel something in your body? What?
- What were your emotions, and where did you feel them in your body?
- What was your internal conversation?
- Did you judge the person who assessed you? What was your assessment of them?
- Did you learn something about the person who made the assessment?

The second condition of validation, unlike with a declaration regarding which you need to take action in order to make the declared thing happen, is to ground the assessment by means of asking yourself five questions:

1. In terms of what future actions are you making the assessment?

You have already seen that when you make an assessment you have a specific concern. You are considering, whether consciously or not, future action.

Let's go back to Damian's twenty-three-year-old teacher. If her future action dealt with starting ballet lessons in order to become a professional dancer, would this woman really be young enough to begin this new career? I more than doubt it. If the future action were that she is going to get married this month, do you think she is too young to get married? You might say yes or no depending on the cultural environment you live in and your own thoughts about youth.

Assessments can be valid for some future actions and not for others.

2. In what domain of action are you making the assessment?

Yesterday I saw a film about a man called Mathew who had retired from Princeton University where he had been an admired and cherished philosophy professor. He met his son at one point in the film, who showed him that he admired Mathew, longed for his love and care, yet never got it. I was struck by the desperation with which Mathew said to his son, "I know I was a lousy father!"

Mathew's colleagues might very well make the following assessment: "Mathew is a great guy." Would his son have agreed? Maybe not. Mathew was great in the academic domain, but not in the parenting one.

A valid assessment in one domain of action might not be so in another.

3. What are your standards for making the assessment?

A standard is something used as a measure, norm, or model in comparative evaluations. You can consider an assessment as a comparative evaluation. When you make one, you are comparing the object of your assessment to your standard. If what you judge is within your standard, the assessment is validated in terms of it. If it is not within your standard, you can assess the object as the opposite. You might be tall or short according to your standard, beautiful or ugly, noisy or quiet, tired or rested, arrogant or humble.

Standards can be personal. This means that not everyone shares the same standards. We can disagree and still all the parties involved might have made valid assessments. Probably Damian and his mother disagree on whether the teacher is young or old, and both of them will have made a valid assessment.

For me this is one of the beauties of assessments. We can disagree if we do not share the same standards. This provides diversity and richness to human life. Now you know what to look for if you want to state the reason for not sharing assessments: check everybody's standards. Then you can decide whether to question others' standards or agree to disagree.

Naturally you cannot set your own standards for all possible assessments. For example, it is not up to you to decide at what age your son can vote in a public election. The standard is age (an assertion in this case), which is mandated by law.

Standards are influenced by historic, social, and cultural norms. If these change, the standards can also change. A woman with a beautiful body in the late 1890s would be considered fat by today's norms. The standard of beauty has been reduced by at least twenty pounds since that date in time. Your personal standards can be greatly influenced by the community in which you live.

Each assessment can have more than one standard. For example, if you assess beauty in the domain of beauty contests, you will find at least five standards: height, weight, hair length, and certain ways of walking and of talking. Notice that standards can be assertions and also assessments.

You can make different valid assessments if your standards are not the same as those of others. For example, innovators and leaders are people who raise current standards or create new ones in their fields of action.

4. What observations (facts, numbers, true assertions) have you made in the past in regard to a kind of action, within your standards, and in the domain of the assessment?

If you are assessing beauty in the domain of a beauty contest, you might observe that the participant's hair falls about two inches lower than her shoulders; she is five feet nine inches tall and weighs 120 pounds; she did not make mistakes when questioned; and she walked in an upright position with her shoulders squared back.

Observations are assertions. Assessments are not observations, but they can be evaluations of observations. It is the observation and not the evaluation that grounds an assessment.

5. Could you make observations that ground the opposite assessment?

Consider Brenda's unpunctuality-at-work story once again. There might be someone who still assesses that Brenda is unpunctual because they did not have the chance to observe

Brenda's change of behavior. It is relevant to consider at what point in time the observations are made.

> - What would you say to someone who assesses Brenda's behavior as unpunctual?

Do Not Confuse Assertions with Assessments

We constantly make assessments. I personally consider that life would be very boring if we only made assertions. Our capacity for learning would be significantly reduced if we did not have the ability to diagnose, evaluate, or judge that "it" is not enough, whatever the "it" is. Unfortunately there are some people who do not know the difference between assertions and assessments. They do not know that only assertions can be true or false since they refer to what is out there in the world. They do not know that they can create new worlds with their words when they make declarations, assessments being among them. These words are not true or false; they are valid or invalid according to the authority to make the assessment and to how well it is grounded.

Can you ground the assessment that you are superior to somebody else just because you say so? Grounding assessments helps us respect one another. It also helps us understand that we need to ask for help and to learn. Assessments are reflective actions, and at the same time they have the power to generate new action.

As you have seen, language presents a pitfall when it expresses speech acts, assertions, and assessments, which are as different as X is from Y.

If you say, "Sarah is four feet tall and weighs one hundred and eighty pounds," you are making an assertion that is very easy to verify as true or false. Supposing it is true, what assessment would you make?

I would make the following assessment: "Sarah is small and overweight." Look at how this last sentence is built. It has the form "Sarah is X and Y." Now look at the assertion above about Sara's height and weight. It also takes the form "Sarah is X (height) and Y (weight)." In this case, X and Y denote completely different aspects about Sarah. The assertion brings the world to us and the word comes after that, whereas the assessment qualifies how Sarah is according to standards that might or might not be shared by others—the word creates the world. The assessment contains facts about Sarah that were observed or measured by someone (height and weight); the assessment is a critical comment that stems from me, not from the world. Your responsibility in making an assertion is to verify the information. We are assuming that has been done in this example. Your responsibility in making an assessment is to have the authority to make it. (In this example, I would have left it as an internal conversation since I do not think I would have had the authority to say it directly to Sarah.) You also need to ground an assessment. You need to consider future action, domain, standards, facts, information, and/or observations to be able to ground it. Standards will vary when you consider whether Sarah can be a good wrestler versus whether she can participate in a beauty contest.

What you have just read might sound very logical, but too often these two very different types of language operations are taken as the same; in most cases they are both taken as assertions. An assertion is information, data; it is what it is. But an assessment can be changed if actions are changed. If Sarah wears heals and reduces her weight, she will probably not be assessed as small and overweight. At any rate, if Sarah does something about her looks it will be due to the assessment that she is small and overweight, and not because of the information about her size and weight.

Take the example of Rose, whose mother repeatedly tells her she is clumsy. Mother and daughter are having a conversation:

M: "Hey, Rose, do you want to help me bake this cake? Come help me, Sweetie, but take care because you know how clumsy you are."

R: "Yes, Mom, I want to learn, but you don't give me the chance. Every time I take out a bowl you rush to grab it away from me while saying I will make a mess."

M: "Maybe, but Honey, I do that because you ARE clumsy. Come on, try and do it right today."

R: "Okay, Mom. What do you want me to do?"

M: "Well, in the first place, don't ask me tons of questions about baking. Oh look. You dropped the spoon! See how clumsy you are?"

R: "Okay, Mom. I'm definitely clumsy. You bake the cake. I need to go and study math anyway."

You can see in this dialogue that "clumsy" is used as an attribute of Rose, as an unchangeable characteristic such as the color of her eyes or her size at birth. The mother uses the word *clumsy* to define her daughter, not to describe a behavior that might be changed with a good attitude from Rose and patience and teaching skills from her mother so that Rose can learn how to bake a cake.

- Do you think this might have consequences in Rose's life?

If mother and child confuse an assessment with an assertion, and they both live it as a part of what and who Rose is, they will undoubtedly create a hidden belief that can play a very important role throughout Rose's life. She might have an aversion to cooking or, on the contrary, become a compulsive cook. Most of the time people are not aware that certain behaviors are conditioned by deeply rooted hidden beliefs that come from listening over and over to assessments taken as assertions. Some of these beliefs become part of your identity, of who you are. Consider that one particular observer who has power over other observers can constitute who you are.

This conditioning works in exactly the same way if the assessment treated as an assertion can be considered positive. Rose will not bake a cake, but she has been taking circus lessons for a while now and has become a skillful acrobat. Her mother is happy about it and tells her friends that her daughter is extraordinary in this area of skill. She can often be heard saying something like, "Rose will never cook because she is clumsy, but you should see what she can do with her body as an acrobat. There's no one like her. Rose, come and show these ladies what you can do!" This can lead to a feeling in Rose that she must be extraordinary. For her it is a mandate from life. One possible consequence is that she will never find satisfaction in what she does because she will find it is not extraordinary enough.

- Can you remember something about you that one of your parents or some other important person in your life repeated over and over again when you were a child?
- Can you relate it to your present life?

If you find a hidden belief and realize that it comes from an assessment and not an assertion, do you think you can change that belief? My answer is that you can change it provided you determine whether you would now give authority to the person who made the assessment and that you ground the assessment. You have the possibility of asking for help in order to change your behavior or you can assess that, according to your standards, there are not enough facts to ground the assessment. You might need to ask yourself if you can change the way you feel about it, knowing that by changing some actions or by invalidating the assessment, a whole new world will be open to you. The nasty observer inside of you who kept the hidden belief in place might lose their power, or might be wise and negotiate with other internal observers who want you to thrive.

Use PEL-MET to produce the change you want. The desired change will be your purpose or objective in this exercise. By repeating this exercise over and over again, you will help yourself create the habit of aligning presence, emotions, and language, and you will discover how to dance with these three gifts in your journey towards fulfillment.

CHAPTER 15

Coordination of Direct Action

Requests and Offers

So far you have seen **declarations** that open or close worlds; **assertions**, which reflect observations you have made in the world; and **assessments**, which qualify what you observe. You have a different responsibility when you make each of these different speech acts.

- What is your responsibility when you make declarations?
- What is your responsibility when you make assertions?
- What is your responsibility when you make assessments?

Now we are going to review three speech acts that deal with direct actions. Through these speech acts people coordinate actions among themselves. As a result of this coordination of actions, new products and artifacts that were one day imagined are designed and come to life, creating a new reality through the activities of specific people.

The three speech acts deal with performance and delivery. They are the conversations that allow us to observe how our culture is changing through the use of technology, what the relationship pattern is between parents and children, what products are consumed, what cities look like, and how people behave in different environments. These are the speech acts that made Kennedy's declaration a valid one: there were millions of requests and offers that turned into millions of fulfilled promises from hundreds of thousands of people who had conversations and did things that created a totally new reality in which twelve people landed on the surface of the moon between 1969 and 1975.[47]

What is a request and what is an offer? When you ask your teenaged son to take out the garbage, you have made a request. When Mary tells her sister Kara that she will take care of Kara's baby when Kara goes out to see her doctor, Mary has made an offer. Something very specific happens when you make a request or an offer (though in the form of a request): you are assessing that something is lacking and is needed in your life. When you want someone else to do what you think is needed, you will make a request. When you yourself intend to provide what is missing, you will make an offer.

---

47. https://www.nasa.gov

COORDINATION OF DIRECT ACTION

When you make a request or an offer, you do so to a specific person. There is a "You" and an "I." You might not know the other person, but they are present.

Yesterday I bought some tablecloths on the Internet. I dialed a phone number that was posted on the website and talked to someone who said, "Hello, my name is . . . . What can I do for you?" I told him what design I had chosen and the measurements of my table, and he said that was all he needed to know. He also added that he would send me a quotation, and as soon as I accepted it he would send the manufacturing order to production. To make a short story even shorter, I accepted the quotation, transferred a deposit, and, as a result, tomorrow I will meet my seller, who will bring me the tablecloths.

Requests and offers have the following form:

I request you to do X in time Y.
I offer you to do M in time N.

If the request or offer is accepted, the person who will take action X or M makes a promise, whether explicit or tacit, with the same form as the request or the offer:

After acceptance of the request or offer, the promise is:

I promise to do X in time Y.
I promise to do M in time N.

X and M are very precise descriptions of what you are requesting or offering. In general, the more precise and detailed you make X and M, the greater the probability of making an effective promise. It is very common to overlook the importance of being precise in what you need (request) or in what you intend to do (offer). This is one of the major causes for customer complaints and misunderstandings between managers and subordinate employees. You think you were very clear because you spoke firmly; nevertheless your very firmness could have caused an emotional reaction of fear, humiliation, or any other for the listener, and their capacity for listening actively might have been reduced. They probably listened to only to part of what you said. On the other hand, you might not have provided all the necessary details if you thought your listener should automatically know what you want. Certainly, if the person has rountinely done what you are asking many times before, it will not be necessary to go into much detail; for both of you, what needs to be done will be obvious. But if you are speaking to someone who is new in the company, that will not be the case. Don't take it for granted that they should know. Be as precise as you possibly can.

Let me give you an example: When at work, if you need someone to write a report on a certain issue, do not hesitate to make a sketch of exactly what you want the report to look like, and specifically what the content should be. (If it is a prescribed report, this will not be necessary.) And if you are the person assigned to write the report, ask about all the possible details before making the promise to write it.

COORDINATION OF DIRECT ACTION

Many years ago I was leading a workshop on these types of speech acts and a woman said, "My husband knows I love violets, and he never buys me any. It really makes me mad."

- Would you have told this woman something? What?

I remember asking a question and having a dialogue like the following with her:

ME: "Ada, have you ever asked your husband to bring you violets?"
A: "No, I don't think so. But I already told you that he knows I like them."
ME: "So he has heard your declaration more than once and has not listened to it as a request."
A: "Shouldn't he?"
ME: "Would you like to try making the request today and see what happens?"
A: "Sure! I'll do that."

Before checking on what happened to Ada's request, we need to address Y and N in the request and offer form depicted above. Y and N express when it is that you want X and M done. Again, the more precise you are in stating the when, the more effective the request or offer will be. Consider at this incident:

Gina and Frank are old friends who have not seen each other for many years. They bump into each other while walking in opposite directions along a street in their hometown. They recognize each other immediately, smile, and chat for a couple of minutes. At the end of the short conversation, Frank waves his hand and says,

F: "It's been wonderful to see you, Gina. Let's have a coffee one of these days so that we can catch up."
G: "That's a great idea, Frank. Let's do it soon."
F: "It's a deal! So long then."

Gina and Frank resume their walking in opposite directions.

- What speech acts were made in the last conversation?
- Do you think Gina and Frank will meet for a coffee?

We frequently have fast conversations that lead to nothing. Without a date and a time, chances are that Gina and Frank will not meet again. Sometimes this type of conversation is used as sheer courtesy without a commitment to meet again. At other times people do not realize until it is too late that they will not reconnect.

Let's go back now to Ada's story. She made a request to her husband the night of our conversation, at dinner:

A: "Manuel, Dear, I have a confession to make."
M: "What? Well, that's news . . . go ahead."
A: "For years I have been a little resentful towards you because you have never bought me violets."
M: "And?"

A: "Well, every time I see a vase of violets I express how I love these flowers. Surely you have heard me say this more than once."

M: "I'm not sure about that. I haven't registered it in my mind."

A: "That's precisely the point of my confession. Apparently I have never asked you to bring violets home, so I have no reason to resent you for not doing so."

M: "Thank you, Ada. It's nice of you to acknowledge it. Give me a kiss!"

Ada gets up and kisses Manuel. When she returns to her chair she says,

A: "Now that this is settled, I want to ask you to please bring me a nice bouquet or two of violets tomorrow when you come home after work."

M: "With pleasure, Dear!"

When I asked Ada how it went with her request, she told the group that she was thrilled and felt as if Manuel and she were dating once again. She said she had been able to test very vividly how reality changes when you make different speech acts.

The declaration "I love violets" was not listened to by Manuel as an action directed towards him. But the request was unavoidably directed towards him, and he was more than happy to accept it and make a promise. From then on Ada almost always had violets at home.

- Is it easy for you to make requests?
- Is it easy for you to make offers?

People often need to get out of their comfort zone in order to make a request or an offer. One reason for this is that it is not possible to take for granted that the request or the offer will be accepted. Without an accepted request or offer, there will be no promise. You might feel rejected, unworthy, or not valued as a person. The invitation here is to acknowledge that the other person can either accept or reject a request or an offer. There is no need to be rude when rejecting a request or an offer. It is not the person who is rejected, but the action that is being proposed.

We have already seen the immense power of language and also the traps that it can make us fall into. If you are aware of the connections between your presence, emotions, and language, aligning them through PEL-MET provides a powerful resource for increasing awareness and bypassing the traps and misunderstandings that often take place in human interaction. One of these traps is to make a promise without previously making the corresponding offer and allowing for its acceptance.

Let's look at a conversation between Diane, who is a single, childless thirty-two-year-old, and her sister Maggie, two years younger than Diane, married to Charles, and the mother of a one-year-old baby:

D: "Maggie, I'm coming on Sunday and will stay the whole day at your place taking care of the baby so you can go out alone with Charles and have fun."

COORDINATION OF DIRECT ACTION

M: "Thanks so much, Sis, but we have plans for Sunday and we shall be taking the baby with us."

D: "Oh, but I thought you and Charles would love this. I already made arrangements with a colleague at work to change my schedule. I am doing this for you, Maggie. I hear you all the time complaining about how busy you are and thought you'd like the break."

M: "When have I complained, Diane? I might say that I am tired sometimes, but complain? I love my baby and I also love taking care of her."

D: "But can't you see all I did in order to be free for you this Sunday?"

M: "I see it and I am sorry, Diane. You should have called me before making the arrangements."

D: "Okay, I see. You don't need me and I will never offer to help you again."

M: "That's not the point. You have been very helpful to us and I am grateful. If you would have made the offer before making the arrangements, I could have thanked you from the bottom of my heart and told you that in two more Saturdays we are having a barbecue at home and it would be wonderful for you to help us with the baby that day."

D: "Oh, we'll see. Now I have to fix the mess you put me in."

M: "I insist, Sister, that if you had called before making formal arrangements, there would be no mess."

D: "Whatever!"

- What happened in this conversation?
- What emotions arose?
- If you had been Diane, would you have done what she did? Why?
- If you had been Maggie, would you have done what she did? Why?

A request or offer can also be responded to with a counteroffer. If someone asks you to do X in time Y, you can say, "Yes, I will do it but in time A," or "I cannot do all of X, but I can do B, and in time C, not Y." Now the person who originally made the request is the one who will have to accept or reject your counteroffer.

I suggest you practice making requests and offers with the help of PEL-MET. When you live with others it is impossible to take care of everything yourself. A request that has been well made can help you increase your power, especially at work. When your X's and Y's are precise, the more requests you make to your collaborators the more you will deliver, provided the members of your team are trained in how important it is to effectively deliver on promises. The more requests you make, the more promises you receive. This means that precise requests have the potential of allowing you to multiply your results. If you can produce and deliver more than others, you will be powerful.

Knowing how to delegate is equivalent to making effective requests. You cannot be a leader or a manager if you do not delegate. On the other hand, talent and expertise are becoming more and more diversified in many industries. This creates a demand for everyone who works in a certain company to make exceptional offers. Today, whether you are an entrepreneur or an employee, you need to know how to delegate and how to make precise offers.

Make a request and an offer that are important to you (in real life):
- You will ask A to do X in time Y.
- You will offer B to do M in time N.
- What was the outcome in each case?
- How did you feel?

There are many verbs that can be used to make requests. I invite you to make a list of them. Different verbs entail different degrees of possible refusal. Check your list and assess how possible it is to say no or to make a counteroffer; that is, change X or Y or both. I call this the "elasticity" of a request, meaning how possible it is to reject the request.

Let us look at some examples:

A group of high school students is working on a test. Suddenly the teacher says, "Time's up! Finish the sentence and hand me your papers!"

- What speech act is this?
- What word best describes this speech act?
- How possible is it to decline what the teacher says?

Two friends have been chatting at a coffee house. They have already paid their check and are ready to leave. Suddenly one says to the other, "By the way, I am having an open house this Friday to meet our classmate Cathy who lives in Australia and is visiting this country. Come by at nine if you wish."

- What speech act is this?
- What word best describes this speech act?
- How possible is it to decline what was just said?

Managing a Promise

You have already seen that only when a request (or an offer) is accepted does it then turn into a promise. Suppose that person Z accepted a request you made, and in turn he made you a promise. The promise has the same form as the request (or an offer).

Request: *I ask you to do X in time Y.*
If the request is accepted:
Promise: You promise *to do X in time Y.*

Offer: *I offer to do M in time N.*
If the offer is accepted:
Promise: *I promise to do M in time N.*

COORDINATION OF DIRECT ACTION

If the person who makes or receives the promise does not understand exactly what is requested or offered, there will surely be misunderstandings. Do you remember how it is possible to improve your listening? In the examples above both the speaker and the listener are responsible for ensuring that they listened to the same X and Y, or M and N. Whether you are the speaker or the listener, be sure to verify exactly what is required or offered, sparing no details. Share your concerns, especially if you are the speaker; inquire or ask questions, especially if you are the listener; until both of you are certain of what the content of the promise is and when it will be fulfilled. You do not want to work for a whole month only to find out that the person who made the request is unhappy with what you did because they think it is not what they requested. Or you, as the person who made the request, will no doubt prefer to ascertain that the person who makes a promise will fulfill it exactly in a certain way and at a time that are perfectly clear to both parties.

Promises are two-stage speech acts. Once a promise is made, taking the precautions above, there is another action that needs to be performed. The promise must be fulfilled. When people talk about employee engagement, they are talking about the disposition of employees to fulfill the promises they make when they sign their contracts. If we're talking about responsible parents of small children, they fulfill the promises they make, whether it be to attend a soccer game in which their child is a player or to go together to buy their child a bike next week, and not today, because Mom is busy now. (This would be an accepted counteroffer made by Mom.)

When you have fulfilled a promise, it is necessary to let the person who made the request, or to whom you made the offer, know that you did so. If they find everything is alright, you can expect a thank you, which you will acknowledge.

- What will happen if you go to the soccer game at the right time, if you buy your daughter a bike next week, if you deliver your promise as requested or as offered?
- What will happen if any of those promises are not fulfilled at the right times?

If your presence, emotions, and language are aligned, you will probably pay attention to the importance of fulfilling your promises in the exact form you made them, doing what you promised and delivering when you promised to do so. This would be enough if we lived in a perfect world. But as you know, unexpected things do happen, and you might have to deal with the fact that you will not deliver X in time Y. In that case, since a promise is time sensitive, you'll need to change the promise or revoke it in its entirety as soon as you can. A very prevalent issue with trust is generated by a delay in letting the interested parties know that you will not fulfill your promise exactly as you made it. I suspect the lack of rigor in such exchanges creates a culture of general mistrust in some countries; like mine, for example.

People do not trust that promises will be fulfilled. This creates the need for activities and worries that would be redundant if we were aware of the difficulties we create when we do not fulfill our promises, or at least revoke them on time, to prevent or reduce the damage that not fulfilling them causes. The way organizations produce their outcomes is through a series of sequential promises. If one of them is broken and corrective measures are not taken in a timely fashion, all the promises that follow will be broken. There is a tremendous collective responsibility in managing your promises at your workplace, since all promises are connected to each other in one way or another. Many disasters could be prevented if promises were explicitly changed or revoked at the right times.

Do You Complain or Whine?

Complaining and whining are two very different actions. Whiners make negative assessments and pour out negative emotions about anything: a world they do not like, someone who has wronged them, the weather—virtually anything. Ultimately they are not expecting to solve a situation with their whining. They only want to grab someone's attention.

When you complain, you have a very different motivation. The greatest difference between whining and complaining is that the root of the complaint is specific: an unfulfilled promise. And the reason to complain is to solve the situation created by the unfulfilled promise. You can be angry when you complain, but the reason to complain is not to express a bad feeling, as is the case for whining, but to find a solution.

Ten days ago I went to the pharmacy in my neighborhood and presented a prescription I needed in preparation for a health test I was going to have the following week. The pharmacist instructed a very young girl, who seemed to me insufficiently trained, to handle the order. The girl entered the data into the computer, called the central lab, and charged me. She took more than thirty minutes to do this, and I was beginning to despair when she finally completed the transaction. I had the following internal conversation (defined in chapter 11) during almost the whole time:

"This poor girl is not trained. She is too young and doesn't seem very clever. What if she makes a mistake? I can't afford this to happen because if the prescription needs to be done again, there won't be enough time before I have to have the test. It's getting late. My next client will have to wait for me. I don't know what to do. This is the problem with this country. Nobody wants to spend money in training. And the stupid pharmacist doesn't give a damn!"

- What was I doing in this conversation?
- Did I do something to solve my concerns?

I might even have grabbed the attention of the people who were at the pharmacy when they saw my desperate face.

Several days later, I went to pick up the prescription. I gave the order to the only person behind the counter. She left the counter and went into an office. Other customers arrived, and there was no one to assist them. The customer standing next to me asked,

COORDINATION OF DIRECT ACTION

C: "Madam, are you also waiting for someone to come to the counter?"

Me: "Actually no, Sir. The only woman who's working behind the counter is processing my order. There must be a problem because she's been gone for almost ten minutes."

The man sighed. This time I began my PEL-MET breathing after noticing some stress in my neck and throat. I did not begin an internal conversation. Five minutes later the employee came to the counter and addressed me:

E: "There's a problem. You were ordered a solution and not a granular preparation, which is what you paid for. The cost is different. We couldn't do anything because we didn't know how to reach you."

Me: "You have all my data in my client file."

E: "Possibly. But we didn't know your name."

At that moment I realized that my internal conversation and my bad mood had not allowed me to think clearly the other day. If I had exercised PEL-MET then, I could have asked myself if my anger was of any use, and I could have decided on an action. I could have insisted on giving the young, untrained girl my name and phone number. This time I said,

Me: "I will pay the extra cost right now. Please tell your boss I need to speak to him."

The employee called her boss out to the counter and I addressed him:

Me: "Sir, I want to know if you agree that I gave the employee a routine order and she made a mistake while entering the data into your computer system."
Boss: "Yes, Madam, I acknowledge this is what happened."
Me: "I also want to know if you understand how this can harm me. There is a possibility of my missing an urgent health test."
Boss: "I am aware of that, Madam."
Me: "In that case, I request that you make an exception and have the prescription prepared for tomorrow without my having to wait the usual eight days."
Boss: "You can come and collect the prescription tomorrow, Madam. I will make arrangements with the central lab to give the utmost priority to this order."
Me: "Thank you."
Boss: "You are welcome. We're very sorry for the inconveniences we caused you."

The next day I went to fetch the prescription and was told it had been prepared the previous day.

Instead of whining and despairing, I made a complaint. I believe it is necessary to complain when a promise is broken. After I show you the conversational structure of a complaint you will see why I think this way.

COORDINATION OF DIRECT ACTION

A complaint is made through the following speech acts:

1. Assertion: I asserted that I gave a routine order. I also asserted that the employee made a mistake. I checked this assertion with the pharmacist.
2. Declaration: I declared that this mistake harmed me and asked if the pharmacist agreed, which he did.
3. Request: I made a new request. By doing so, I opened a door to regain lost trust and to interact again.

Complaints end when the person who broke the promise accepts a new request. Making a request leads to the possibility of continuing an interaction that without it will remain closed. It is possible that if I had not complained, my prescription would not have been ready in time for the health test. I would either have suffered from an emotion of indignity if I continued to go to that pharmacy, or I would have had to find another pharmacy, which would definitely have been located farther away, with the corresponding inconvenience.

Think about a complaint you would like to make and still have not.
- Do you feel something in your body when you recall the situation?
- Name the emotion you feel.
- Make the complaint. If possible, do so in real life.
- How did you feel after making the complaint?

We have said that in order to regain the possibility of interaction, a complaint must be made. The complaint has a specific structure ending with a request. This request is an indication that you are willing to give trust and the relationship a second chance.

There is another reason to complain. If someone breaks a promise they made to you without letting you know in advance, you will probably feel that they are taking you for granted, showing an utter lack of respect for the person that you are. Such a situation affects your dignity. The only way to recover it is by complaining. You need to become an expert in distinguishing whining from complaining. The only way to solve a situation is to give it a new chance by making a request as the last speech act of the complaint. Only then will your dignity be safeguarded.

CHAPTER 16

Trust

A Widely Used Term that Is Difficult to Define

Are you well acquainted with the word *trust*? I bet you are. There are hundreds of books with this word in their titles, and there is a great deal of training offered on this topic, especially in regard to marriage and corporate team-building. Several management and leadership models place it as the single most important issue to address in order to improve bottom-line results and the well-being of employees.

To me trust is like intuition: something you know you know, but that you cannot easily define. I think one of the reasons for this is that trust is both emotional and logical.

Cynthia, thirteen years old, was granted permission for the first time in her life to come back home no later than 11:00 p.m. by her own means. Her mother waited for her at the door before Cynthia left the house.

Mom: "Cynthia, Dear, we can still change our minds. Are you completely sure that you don't want me to pick you up at eleven? Just tell me where."
C: "Mom, please, I'm not a baby!"
Mom: "Sorry, Darling. I worry. Dad and I just want you to be safe."
C: "Well then, do you think I cannot take care of myself?"
Mom: "No, Sweetheart, it's not that. It's just that you've never done this before, and being out this late at night might be dangerous."
C: "You know me well, Mom. I won't do anything silly. Trust me!"

Cynthia kisses her mom and leaves.

- What did you listen to in this conversation?
- How did Mom relate to trust?
- How did Cynthia relate to trust?
- How would you have related to trust in this conversation?

In my understanding, Cynthia's mom had an issue with trust, both emotionally and logically. She was afraid that something could happen to her daughter, whatever her age or the circumstances. This is an expression of her distrust of the environment that might not have been verbalized before, in which case she would be dealing with an emotional distrust. Mom had probably already put into words the thought of this being a first experience for her daughter, and her assessment probably was that Cynthia might be too young to handle the responsibility. So to a possible emotional distrust, a logical one was added. This is a common trust issue between teenagers and their parents. If handled well, it can become a learning experience for everyone. If not, it can cause resentment.

The experience of trust, or the lack of it, is always present in relationships. It can arise from emotions, feelings, and moods, either with or without awareness. Family and social conditioning may can inadvertently influence trust in a relationship. As a child you might have been told:

"Don't trust strangers!"
"You can trust people who play musical instruments. They are sensitive."
"Men should not be trusted."
"Women cannot be trusted to make good, tough decisions."

These are general, invalid assessments taught and received as assertions. You might not be aware of this conditioning. You might have an unconscious positive attitude towards musicians and yet feel scared in front of strangers. Usually this kind of conditioning creates an emotional approach to trust.

- Explore what you might have been told that created an attitude, feeling, or mood in relation to trust.

The logical aspect of trust deals with promises and specific assessments. You have seen in the last chapter how breaking promises affects trust. In order to be able to interact, you need to trust. That is why it is so important to complain when a promise is not well performed or is broken. You lose trust in a person who broke a promise. As a consequence, as long as there is no trust, the relationship with this person will be broken. The only way you can reactivate it is by giving trust a second chance. In a complaint, the request with which you finish it is a speech act that allows you to rebuild the lost trust, or part of it.

What do I mean when I relate the logical aspect of trust to specific assessments? Since it is never obvious whether you can trust someone or not, especially if you do not know the person very well, you can assess four types of behaviors in order to determine whether or not to trust them, provided there has been some sort of interaction between you. Before doing that let's review the dialogue between Cynthia and her mother and answer the following questions:

- Does Mom believe what Cynthia said to her?
- What thoughts led you to your answer to the previous question?
- Did Mom have any doubts about Cynthia's capacity to face unexpected situations?

- What thoughts led you to your answer to the previous question?
- Does Mom consider that Cynthia usually keeps her promises?
- What thoughts led you to your answer to the previous question?
- Does Mom consider that her daughter might be too exposed to danger when she walks alone at night?
- What thoughts led you to your answer to the previous question?

If you have doubts about trusting someone, make assessments based on the person's:

- **Sincerity**: What they say to themselves about an issue is the same as what they say to anybody else. In other words, they are not lying.
- **Competences:** They have proven skills to do what they intend to.
- **Reliability:** They have a record of kept promises.
- **Vulnerability**: They are open to expressing their feelings and emotions in order not to be exposed to a risky situation.

Now go back to the questions above and establish how your answers relate to these four assessments. Check if your answers to the questions are the same now as they were before reading about the four traits that help you treat trust as a logical issue with four assessments.

Quite frankly, I think it is not easy to deal with the assumption or, even worse, the confirmation that you have been lied to. In fact, I am now wrestling with a decision I need to make after discovering that someone I put my trust in at work had pretended to hear what I told him and to be empathic. I later discovered that he had known about the issue I brought up beforehand, and that what he said to me were lies. I am taking my time in responding because he is not the only one involved and it might mean that I have to step aside from an exciting project. This is a humbling experience for me.

- Have you lied as a self-defensive strategy?
- If yes, what have you gained and what have you lost?
- Have you been lied to?
- What did you do after you discovered that you were lied to?
- How do you relate to lying and to being trusted?
- How do you relate to trusting and being lied to?

Cynthia's mom probably trusted Cynthia's sincerity, but not her competence in dealing with unexpected situations while strolling the streets at night. She probably understood that there is always a first time for every experience, and that her daughter needed to take special precautions precisely because she had not yet had the experience that would have provided the needed competence.

People can be sincere and have the competence to make a promise, but have a history of unkept ones that prevents others from trusting them.

Vulnerability is a two-way issue: assessing that someone is vulnerable can be favorable in certain situations and unfavorable in others. If you were the CEO of a company that is having great financial difficulties, and you need to fire a percentage of the employees, you would most likely utilize for the task someone in the firm whom you have assessed as vulnerable and open to expressing their emotions. They would communicate the termination of jobs to each of the affected employees in an empathic way. You could trust this person to help reduce the suffering that losing a job can cause.

On the other hand, if you are the same CEO and a significant theft has just been discovered, you are not going to send someone vulnerable to emotional distress to handle the situation. In that case vulnerability is a disadvantage.

Trust, as said, is an inseparable attribute of any relationship. There will always be someone who trusts more or less, and someone who is more or less trustworthy. In some relationships all parties trust and at the same time are trustworthy in varying degrees. Behavior, though, is the result of different elements when someone is trusting than when they are being trustworthy. You do not take the same kinds of actions when you trust that you do when you are being trustworthy. Now when you consider trusting someone you will make the four assessments — sincerity, competence, reliability, and vulnerability. And when you are the one who must be trusted, you will evaluate your own trustworthiness and also predict how the other person will assess you. Use your intuition to judge whether or not your counterpart has any emotional issues concerning your trustworthiness, then ask yourself if your behavior allows them to positively assess your sincerity, competence, reliability, and vulnerability in the context of your relationship.

Have you noticed that when a concept is difficult to define you often bump into diverse definitions and not all of them mean the same thing? This is the case with trust. "It has been defined as both a noun and a verb, as both a personality trait and a belief, and as both a social structure and a behavioral intention. Some researchers, silently affirming the difficulty of defining trust, have declined to define it, relying on the reader to ascribe meaning to the term."[48]

Trust and Distrust

Trust and distrust are two distinct opposites that usually coexist. Rarely do we find absolute trust or absolute distrust. If we do it generally means that we're dealing with dysfunctional behavior.

You need at least a certain level of trust just in order to interact with another. Human beings live with and among other human beings, so interaction is inescapable. This means that trust is inescapable. If someone does not trust anyone, at

---

48. D. H. McKnight and N. L. Chervany, "Trust and Distrust Definitions: One Bite at a Time," joint essay, Michigan State University and University of Minnesota, 2001.

any level at all, they are possibly demonstrating pathological emotional distrust. This behavior escapes the scope of this book, and you would probably turn away from a relationship in which you observe it.

On the other hand, if someone has no distrust towards you whatsoever, they are probably denying facts in order to accommodate your desires. When you fall in love, especially if it is love at first sight, you usually imagine that all facts fit your fantasy. There is an expression that summarizes this state of being: blind love. My experience and understanding is that love is infinite as a possibility, which is why I would change that expression to a somewhat less romantic one: blind trust. Even if your lover's actual behavior contradicts your assumptions, you will continue trusting them, like a baby trusts its mother regardless of her actions. That is why your behavior is named naiveté, childlikeness, or innocence. Such attitudes and behaviors are attributed to very young infants.

If you behave naively, you become untrustworthy to others. It is clear to the people with whom you interact that you tend to omit facts that others consider important, turning you into someone who could be dangerous. Innocence is appropriate in young children, but not in adults.

The suggestion then is this: Beware of complete emotional distrust and of total innocence! If that is valid, what is left?

Adults can exercise prudence. An attitude of prudence means that you admit there might be a need for a certain amount of distrust in a trusting environment. In other words, distrust-related behavior means that when negative consequences are possible, you do not voluntarily depend with total confidence on another person.

The simultaneous interplay of trust and distrust is evident in the diplomatic arena. What follows is part of a declaration between the United States, Russia, and other countries made in October of 2015, regarding the Syrian confrontation:

> "The United States and Russia are prepared, in their capacities as co-chairs of the Ceasefire Task Force and in coordination with other members of the ISSG[49] Ceasefire Task Force as appropriate, to develop effective mechanisms to promote and monitor compliance with the ceasefire both by the governmental forces of the Syrian Arab Republic and other forces supporting them, and the armed opposition groups. To achieve this goal and to promote an effective and sustainable cessation of hostilities, the Russian Federation and the United States will establish a communication hotline and, if necessary and appropriate, a working group to exchange relevant information after the cessation of hostilities has gone into effect."[50]

Just think about what kind of chaos the world would be in if some of the most powerful countries in the world, adversaries in many ways, did not create windows of trust and precautions of distrust to maintain order on our planet!

---

49. CSSG: International Syrian Support Group co-chaired by the US and Russia, created in October of 2015.
50. http://www.state.gov/r/pa/prs/ps/2016/02/253115.htm

In the field of business, the simultaneous need for both trust and distrust simultaneously is easy to observe. Imagine you are an auditing manager of a large consulting firm, and a CEO who suspects internal fraud by some of her firm's executives hires your firm to audit her own. Inadvertently you send an auditor with high interpersonal trust and low interpersonal distrust to handle the job. They might tend to ignore evidence that supports not trusting the executives. If there was fraud, this auditor might not detect it. And just as love is sometimes blind, a very trusting auditor might be blind to negative traits of the executives. But when a healthy dose of distrust exists, there is a possibility for the auditor to be more attentive to negative traits and to more easily find problems that need to be solved.

On the other hand, if trust and distrust are not well balanced, and if furthermore there is a power differential between the parties, they will not be able to reconcile with each other, even to the point of not cooperating. Action will be paralyzed.

An appropriate combination of trust and distrust is desirable in every area of our lives. You saw that Cynthia's mother trusted her in general, yet had some distrust at the same time. Think about marriage, friendship, love relationships, business, teams, or any other circumstance in which humans coexist.

On a scale of one to ten:
- How much trust and how much distrust do you need at work?

> - How much trust and how much distrust do you need at home (with a spouse, parents, roommate(s) or children)?

The Impact of Forgiveness

Have you ever forgiven someone or been forgiven for something said or done? Forgiveness can be a powerful declaration that lays the groundwork for restoring trust.

You need to forgive someone or yourself if the actions that you will forgive (or the lack of them) caused negative emotions or suffering that turned into moods. Bad feelings persisted and you probably felt enraged for a long time. Or maybe that feeling never disappeared and turned into resentment, which is ready to pop out with any dissatisfaction. You might even live with a hidden desire for revenge. Here is an example of how these feelings can occur:

Karen and her friends went out to eat at a restaurant. Karen ordered a glass of sparkling wine and her friends ordered beer. The waiter gave Karen a glass of wine in which she could not identify a single spark or hint of fizz. She serenely asked for a replacement from the server and returned it to him. She ended her complaint by asking the server if he could be sure to bring sparkling wine to the table the next time around. The waiter replied, "Certainly, Ma'am!" Within a short time Karen received what she wanted.

- Did Karen act appropriately with the waiter?
- What thoughts motivated your answer?
- Was there a need for someone to forgive someone else?

In this case ending the complaint with a request was enough to restore trust. The result was that the incident was almost unnoticed by Karen's friends and she had a great time at the restaurant.

As said, you forgive when there is an important emotional component. Forgiveness allows you to let go of your suffering. It has much more to do with your own well-being than with that of the person you forgive. When you hold on to suffering — whether it is resentment, hurt, or anger — you turn inward, feel powerless, and victimize yourself, expressing self-pity. This is how you start to see the world, with the eyes of a victim. You feel the need to punish the transgressor, so it is important for you to keep those bad moods alive, otherwise you will not show how deeply you were hurt. You cannot escape from suffering. Please notice how closely related rage and victimhood are.

Forgiving someone is very different from forgetting their despicable actions and the damage they produced. The memory of the incident and the damage it created will probably stay with you always. Forgiveness is a decision to stop carrying the burden of your victimization. Forgiveness is relaxing from bad feelings and opening to a different way to perceive the world and your place in it. You decide if you will create a window of trust or continue to totally distrust the person who harmed you; if you do the latter, you will not relate to them any longer, which is your legitimate choice, but nevertheless you will break the ties that your suffering and desire for revenge had created and maintained. What a relief!

- Have you forgiven someone?
- What happened between you after forgiveness?
- How did you feel?
- Have you been forgiven?
- What happened between you after forgiveness?
- How did you feel?

Trusting and Distrusting Organizational Cultures

The development of science and engineering that took place during the eighteenth and nineteenth centuries changed completely the context of labor and the structure of organizations, demanding massive production. In 1890, companies employed a small number of workers. Only twenty-five years later, in 1915, companies like U.S. Steel and Ford Motor Company employed thousands of workers. A new organizational paradigm had to be put in place. Productivity and efficiency are the greatest requirements of mass production. The human quality of learning that existed beforehand in the apprenticeship system had to be replaced by the availability of masses of untrained workers who only had to make small physical movements in huge production lines. Frederick Taylor, to whom the first modern paradigm owes its name, said:

"We do not ask our men for initiative. We don't want initiative. We want them to do what we tell them to, and fast!"[51]

The model was extremely successful. It increased productivity and efficiency to unimaginable levels. The Taylor paradigm is still used in many companies and organizations in the world, sometimes coexisting with others. On one hand there are engineers who determine what must be done and how, and on the other there are workers who obey instructions. A new structural level had to be created in between: foremanship. Foremen supervise the work of workers and lower-level foremen. This type of supervision is exercised by infusing fear among the workers. At the time the model was implemented, workers could be fired if they did not produce at the required speed, and there would be a monetary incentive in cases in which productivity was greater than specifically required by the engineers, though such incentive has not been widely put in place.

Summarizing, the Taylor paradigm functions on the basis of workers' fear. This leads to an organizational culture based on fear regardless of whether there is awareness of the situation on the part of employees.

- What kind of organizational culture can you expect from Taylor's paradigm: trustful or distrustful?

---

51. Rafael Echeverría, *La Empresa Emergente*, Granica eds., 2000

By the mid-twentieth century, other management paradigms had been born. Peter Drucker introduced the paradigm of effectiveness, quality, and knowledge *circa* 1960. He stated that knowledge is even more important than raw materials. He also said that quality is more important than quantity. Drucker is still frequently quoted in regard to his thoughts on effectiveness. The following is an example:

"There is nothing as useless as doing efficiently that which should not be done at all."[52]

From then on, very slowly but surely, management paradigms shifted more and more to highlighting the importance of people all levels of an organization. Today knowledge is considered a commodity since it can be easily found on the World Wide Web, hired, or bought. What the future demands is a set of human qualities: community, interdependence, freedom, flexibility, transparency, meritocracy, self-determination, vision, creativity, passion, and adaptability.

Gary Hamel was ranked by *The Wall Street Journal* in 2015 as the world's most influential business thinker. His aim is "to build organizations that are fit for the future and fit for human beings."[53] Hamel, other business thinkers, and several high-level corporate executives are intent on changing organizational cultures from fear to trust as the only way to advance in the direction of building companies fit for the future and for human

---

52. Peter Drucker, (n.d.) BrainyQuote.com. Retrieved April 6, 2016, from BrainyQuote.com: http://www.brainyquote.com/quotes/quotes/p/peter-druck105338.html
53. https://www.youtube.com/watch?v=aodjgkv65MM

beings. The tools provided in this chapter will help you, your partners, your bosses, and your collaborators determine the proportion of distrust needed in your business relations.

During the last decade of the past century there was a sudden increase in the exchange of knowledge, trade, and capital around the world, driven by technological innovation in everything from the Internet to shipping containers. This fact is greatly responsible for the explosive appearance of the term *globalization*. Due to globalization, many large companies such as Philips were compelled to make a huge effort to change their organizational cultures from fear to trust. "The 1990s was a decade of significant change for Philips as the company simplified its structure and reduced the number of areas in which it operated."[54] Decision-making in a global world cannot be centralized. There is no time for that. In the early nineties Philips had to change fast or die, as did several other companies.

A trusting culture is crucial for using the talents of all the members of an organization, for creating leaders at all levels, and for generating engagement and well-being. Keep in mind that the only way your company will be able to build a trusting culture is through the involvement and commitment of those at the highest ranks in the organization, starting with the president and including all other members of the board, the CEO, and the rest of the executives, and considering each and every one of them.

---

54. http://www.philips.com/a-w/about/company/our-heritage.html

Building Self-Confidence

This section is the last one of this chapter. Nevertheless, it is the first section you will deal with when addressing the issue of trust. It is a basic requirement for your journey towards fulfillment.

Let us first distinguish self-confidence from self-esteem. Self-esteem is a basic requirement for living a good life. It refers to the person that you are, not necessarily to specific actions that you do. In order to assess whether you have the self-esteem needed to start your journey, I suggest you observe the observers in you and determine if there is one or more who need to be silenced because they intend to sabotage your initiatives through utterances such as *Since when do you think you are capable of . . . ?*; fill you with fear of being afraid; or make moves that will exhaust your drive to enter into an uncomfortable zone in order to reach fulfillment later.

Check your strengths and correlate them to your self-esteem. You might not even know that it is low in terms of your strengths. This might help you change the way you are feeling in the present moment. PEL-MET is an excellent tool for increasing your self-esteem. If the ultimate purpose is fulfillment, doing things to increase your self-esteem is much more valuable than consuming a lot of energy trying to understand why it is lower than you want it to be. After all, you now know that understanding is no more and no less than making an interpretation, or in other words, building a story that makes sense to you.

Self-confidence relates to your skills, not to your whole being. If you consider yourself a poor skier, your self-confidence will be low in sports such as skiing. At the same time your self-confidence in the area of public speaking might be very high. Self-confidence can be seen as equivalent to trust. The same tools you learned for building trust and distrust are the ones you will use to assess yourself and ground your assessment, or to check your moods and feelings, depending on whether the need to improve your self-confidence has an emotional or a logical root.

- In what areas are you self-confident?
- In what areas are you self-distrustful?
- In what areas are you going to increase your self-confidence?
- What will you do to achieve the self-confidence you would like? (List actions you will take in each area you want to improve.)

It is essential for the novel entrepreneur to clarify their levels of self-esteem and self-confidence in the required fields in order to start their enterprise and then make it flourish. Self-esteem and self-confidence are extraordinary tools for the journey towards fulfillment.

CHAPTER 17

Why the Latest Findings in Neuroscience Matter!

Taking a Look at the Human Brain

The human brain is considered the most complex structure in the universe. It weighs three pounds on average and contains 100 billion neurons. This number is equivalent to the stars in our Milky Way galaxy plus the number of galaxies in the known universe.[55]

A neuron is an electrically excitable cell that processes and transmits information via electrochemical signaling through

---

55. http://www.dummies.com/how-to/content/neuroscience-for-dummies-cheat-sheet.html

what is called a synaptic connection. Each neuron can be connected to up to 10,000 other neurons passing signals to each other via as many as 1,000 trillion synaptic connections, equivalent by some estimates to a computer with a one-trillion-bit-per-second processor.[56]

It is not difficult to understand why there is still so much to learn about this important and mysterious organ, but its study is a process that is moving fast. There have been huge breakthroughs in neuroscience during the last thirty years and more are expected in the near future. Many of the findings provide knowledge about human behavior, the relationship between people and their environment, and the operation of learning, which, as you have seen, are relevant topics throughout this book. I am really fascinated by the discovery that while learning changes behavior it effectively changes our brain, not only in terms of new connections and pathways within it, but also anatomically. This extraordinary ability of the brain to modify its own structure and functions following changes in the body or in the external environment is called *brain plasticity*.

Drs. Arvid Carlsson, Paul Greengard, and Eric Kandel received the Nobel Prize in Physiology or Medicine in 2000 for their discoveries concerning "signal transduction in the nervous system."[57] Kandel describes his lifelong findings, including the effect of learning on the brain, in his book *In Search of Memory*.[58] This book triggered my awareness that through learning we can overcome unwanted and no longer necessary survival

---

56. http://www.human-memory.net/brain_neurons.html
57. https://www.nobelprize.org/nobel_prizes/medicine/laureates/2000/press.html
58. Eric Kandel, *In Search of Memory*, W. W. Norton, 2006.

behaviors on behalf of building fulfilling paths for our personal and collective lives.

The human brain, as we know it today, has been compared to a city with a long history. It has its old sections where in ancient times the activities required for survival took place. It has other, newer sections that developed around the older ones. And it also has a modern section, as we know it now, which was built on the foundations of the other sections and is constantly creating connections among all of them.

An efficient model for understanding the brain with this approach is the triune brain theory developed in 1970 by Paul MacLean.[59] According to this theory, the following three distinct brains emerged in succession during the course of evolution and now coinhabit and interact within the human skull. In a bottom-up sequence, which coincides with the evolutionary states, we find the reptilian, limbic, and neo-cortex brains.

The reptilian brain, the oldest of the three, controls the body's vital functions such as heart rate, breathing, body temperature, and balance. Our reptilian brain includes the main structures found in a reptile's brain: the brainstem and the cerebellum. The reptilian brain is reliable, but tends to be somewhat rigid and compulsive, with little or no place at all for choice.

The limbic system is the portion of the brain that deals with three key functions: emotions, memories, and arousal (stimulation). It connects parts of the brain that deal with high and low functions. Because of these connections, it is

---

59. "The Brain from Top to Bottom:" http://thebrain.mcgill.ca/flash/d/d_05_cr/d_05_cr_her/d_05_cr_her.html

related to unconscious value systems that exert a strong influence on our behavior. The main structures of the limbic brain are the hypothalamus, the amygdala, and the hippocampus.

The hypothalamus is responsible for producing chemical messengers, which we know as hormones. They control water levels in the body, sleep cycles, body temperature, and food intake.

The amygdala is responsible for preparing the body for emergency situations such as being startled, and for storing memories of events for future recognition. It contributes to the development of memories, particularly as it relates to emotional events and emergencies. The amygdala is also involved specifically in the development of the emotion of fear, and it plays a major role in pleasure and sexual arousal.

The hippocampus is responsible for converting short-term memories into long-term ones. It is thought to work with the amygdala on memory storage. Damage to the hippocampus can lead to amnesia (memory loss).

In 2014, John O'Keefe and the team of May-Britt Moser and Edvard I. Moser received the Nobel Prize in Physiology or Medicine for their discoveries of cells that constitute a positioning system in the brain, a sort of "inner GPS" that makes it possible to orient ourselves in space. In 1971, O'Keefe discovered the first component of this positioning system when he observed that the hippocampus was always activated when a rat was at a certain place in a room. Other nerve cells were activated when the rat was at other places. O'Keefe concluded that these "place cells" formed a map of the room.

The neocortex, or the "newest" brain, is involved in higher-order brain functions such as sensory perception, cognition, generation of motor commands, spatial reasoning, and language. It first assumed importance in primates, and culminated in the human brain with its two large cerebral hemispheres, which play a very dominant role. These hemispheres are responsible for the development of human language, abstract thought, imagination, and consciousness. The neo-cortex is flexible, so it has the power of choice and also the capacity for almost infinite learning. Human cultures owe their development to the neocortex. The prefrontal cortex, which is the anterior part of the neocortex, has the role of planning complex cognitive behavior, personality expression, decision- making, and moderating social behavior.[60]

Recent studies show that humans' superior abilities to anticipate and plan in regard to other mammals, especially primates, who are the most similar to humans, can be more correctly attributed to several specialized regions of the cortex and to denser interconnections between the prefrontal cortex and the rest of the brain than to the prefrontal cortex itself, whose size is similar in humans and some primates.[61]

The New Science of Mind

In his book *In Search of Memory*, referenced at the beginning of this chapter, Kandel[62] proposes the emergence of a new science of mind consisting of a combination of neuroscience,

---

60. http://www.goodtherapy.org/blog/psychpedia/prefrontal-cortex
61. https://sites.google.com/site/systemsneurolaboratory/prefrontal-cortex
62. Kandel's Nobel Prize speech: http://www.nobelprize.org/nobel_prizes/medicine/laureates/2000/kandel-lecture.pdf

molecular biology, and cognitive psychology. Kandel wrote in the 2011 edition of the book:

"Indeed, when intellectual historians look back on the last two decades of the twentieth century, they are likely to comment on the surprising fact that the most valuable insights into the human mind to emerge during this period did not come from the disciplines traditionally concerned with mind—from philosophy, psychology, or psychoanalysis. Instead, they came from a merger of these disciplines with the biology of the brain, a new synthesis energized recently by the dramatic achievements in molecular biology. The result has been a new science of mind, a science that uses the power of molecular biology to examine the great remaining mysteries of life."[63]

Kandel is enthusiastic about the plasticity of the brain and its power to answer many questions that had not been asked before in the domain of biology but have been food for thought in philosophy and spirituality for ages. The enormous number, variety, and interactions of the nerve cells in the brain allow the new science of mind to address questions like: How does the mind acquire knowledge of the world? How much of our mind is inherited? Do innate mental functions impose on us a fixed way of experiencing the world? What physical changes occur in the brain as we learn and remember? How is an experience that lasts minutes converted to a lifelong memory? Today all these questions can be asked in the area of experimental research.

---

63. Kandel, *In Search of Memory*.

WHY THE LATEST FINDINGS IN NEUROSCIENCE MATTER!

This new science is based on five principles, Kandel explains. First, mind and brain are inseparable. (Keep in mind that until now many accepted Cartesian dualism, or the separation of the mind and the body. PEL-MET, among others processes, shows that they are inseparable.) The brain is a complex biological organ of great computational capability that constructs our sensory experiences, regulates our thoughts and emotions, and controls our actions. The brain is responsible not only for relatively simple motor behaviors such as running and eating, but also for the complex acts that you and I consider quintessentially human, such as thinking, speaking, and creating works of art. Viewed from this perspective, the mind is a set of operations carried out by the brain, much as walking is a set of operations carried out by the legs. The difference between them is that the operations of the brain are dramatically more complex.

Second, specialized neural circuits in different regions of the brain carry out each mental function in the brain—from the simplest reflex to the most creative acts in language, music, and art. This is why it is preferable to use the term *biology of mind* to refer to the set of mental operations carried out by these specialized neural circuits rather than *biology of the mind*, which connotes a place and implies a single brain location that carries out all mental operations.

Third, all of these circuits are made up of the same elementary signaling units: the nerve cells or neurons.

Fourth, the neural circuits use specific molecules to generate signals within and between nerve cells.

Finally, these specific signaling molecules have been conserved—retained, as it were—through millions of years of evolution. Some of them were present in the cells of our most ancient ancestors and can be found today in our most distant and primitive evolutionary relatives: single-celled organisms such as bacteria and yeast, and simple multicellular organisms such as worms, flies, and snails. These creatures use the same molecules to organize maneuvering through their environment that we use to govern our daily lives and adjust to our environment. Thus we gain from the new science of mind not only insights into ourselves—how we perceive, learn, remember, feel, and act—but also a new perspective of ourselves in the context of biological evolution. It makes us appreciate that the human mind evolved from molecules used by our lowly ancestors, and that the extraordinary conservation of the molecular mechanisms that regulate life's various processes also applies to our mental life.

- What possibilities are opening for human beings to live in a desired world?
- What limitations will prevail and how will they affect human action?

Brain's Action Affects Your Life

Mark Robert Waldman devoted his professional life to the study of mental health and human consciousness in order to understand how our brain influences our life. During the last ten years he has worked full time in neuroscience trying to discover what he calls the secret to happiness and success. He has reviewed hundreds of thousands of studies, summarizing his conclusion as follows:

> *"Life is simple, and satisfaction is easy to attain, but the human mind is blind to this fundamental truth."*[64]

Waldman tells us that our senses collect information about the outside world and our brain processes it in ways to enhance our survival. Once again you can observe an evolutionary approach in this viewpoint.

According to Waldman, as you go up the evolutionary ladder brains become more complex and more sensory organs are built around it. Each organ (eyes, nose, tongue, ears) is specialized and responds to the world in a different way. But the part of the brain that processes the information is in our frontal cortex, and the sensory centers send little information to it, so what we see is more like a movie that blends light, sound waves, and inner emotional experiences into a story that is far removed from the reality from where the sensory organs took their information.

The part of the frontal cortex that processes a limited and complex amount of information is what Waldman calls our mind. (The notion of mind as part of the brain, just as Kandel's science of mind, is 180 degrees away from that of René Descartes, still considered by many scholars as the father of modern Western philosophy. For this mathematician and

---

64. Mark R. Waldman, *10 Mind-Blowing Discoveries about the Human Brain*, 2014.

philosopher, mind and body were two separate entities that interacted with one another.[65])

In the brain, says Waldman, this process happens in a very tiny area of the frontal lobe, the part that makes us aware of ourselves and of the choices we make. He calls it the conscious brain. Consciousness cannot hold much information in working memory during a brief time. We might have the illusion that we are conscious of many things at the same time: colors, movement around us, awareness of our goals, and so on; but that is not so. We can only be aware of a tiny bit of information at a time. Try to remember a sentence with ten words that somebody said very recently. Or try to recall, without looking of course, the last sentence you read before this one. Do not be sad about the probable result of your inquiry, since it has benefits.

For example, you cannot focus on a positive experience or memory and a negative experience or memory at the same time. What does this mean? That if you are feeling pain, the sensation of it will decrease if you do something pleasurable. I invite you to try this exercise whenever you feel uneasy, or are suffering or in pain: Bring forth an agreeable memory or do something you like to do to remove the hurtful sensation. (PEL-MET is with us once again.) If the negative feelings you are experiencing are not caused by an event that happened just now, those feelings come from memories, which are not truths but subjective elaborations. They are combinations of various facts and interpretations that might not even have taken place at the same time. And these memories can

---

65. Internet Encyclopedia of Philosophy, "René Descartes: The Mind-Body Distinction," http://www.iep.utm.edu/descmind/#H4

contain negative feelings that are brought out as if they were present emotions.

Waldman was challenged by a question he was asked during an interview that took place in 2013. After a year he produced his own version of the ten most mind-blowing discoveries about the human brain. And guess what? One of his discoveries was that the brain has a preference to embed negative memories. (Do you remember we went through this issue in chapter 3?) His explanation is that our organism needs to respond to future threats faster than our conscious mind can respond. If you see someone driving a car into your lane on the highway, the consciousness in the frontal lobe is turned down so that your instinctual reactiveness can take evasive action. "This is like a more ancestral form of awareness that takes over the body's control," said Waldman.

I think that probably the limbic system is the structure taking over. This primitive awareness is stored in your memory and your brain responds to it later as if it were a real threat occurring in the present moment. Keep in mind that memories are inaccurate, and each time they are recalled they are slightly changed.

Predominance of Bad over Good

Recall that the brain is more susceptible to grasping bad information than good. According to Waldman, the more you ruminate on the possibility that something awful will happen, the more your brain releases stress chemicals to prepare your body for the fight-or-flight response. When your brain sees that there is no real threat it releases more stress chemicals as a result of confusion. This is a sure way to damage your brain and a good reason to learn to break unhealthy habits and create newer, healthier ones.

Stanford University professor Clifford Nass said, "The brain handles positive and negative information in different hemispheres. Negative emotions generally involve more thinking, and the information is processed more thoroughly than in the case of positive emotions. Thus, we tend to ruminate more about unpleasant events—and use stronger words to describe them—than happy ones."[66]

Nass and Waldman observed the same phenomenon but explained it somewhat differently. Nass did not intend to solve the negativity issue, whereas Waldman's interest in neuroscience appears to be rooted in his desire to know how to reach satisfaction and success.

Since consciousness is limited, as Waldman tells us, you can ruminate on negativity or focus on solution-based goals, but you cannot do both. You have to choose. Your way to awareness is up to you. It is your decision and your responsibility. You have the capacity to consciously train your brain to interrupt negativity and introduce optimism into your life.

If you choose to be aware of yourself, you will also be able to interact with others by paying attention to the good and bad comments you make. It has been established, as you have already read in a previous chapter, that your ideal way of

---

66. http://www.nytimes.com/2012/03/24/your-money/why-people-remember-negative-events-more-than-positive-ones.html?mcubz=3.

communicating with someone includes five positive comments for each negative one you make. I also suggest that you deliver bad news before good news, provided you are certain that the negative emotions that might surge can be well handled so that the aftertaste of the conversation will be nice and sweet.

Consequences of Neuroplasticity

As you have already seen, not only the structure of the brain is important in defining who we are and what we do, but also the huge number of structural and functional connections that the neurons are able to create. That is why I think it is worthwhile to take a deeper look at neuroplasticity. Some authors have defined it as the selective organizing of connections between neurons in our brains.[67] This means that when people repeatedly practice an activity or access a memory, their neural networks—groups of neurons that fire together, creating electrochemical pathways—shape themselves according to that activity or memory. Kandel observed this in the twentieth century.

When people stop practicing new things, their brains eventually eliminate, or "prune" the connecting cells that formed the pathways. Imagine a system of freeways connecting various cities. The more cars going to a certain destination, the wider the road that carries them needs to be. However, the fewer cars traveling that way, the fewer the lanes that are needed. In learning, neuroplasticity allows for changes in the neural connections and even in the anatomy of the brain.

---

[67]. Sarah Bernard, "Neuroplasticity: Learning Physically Changes the Brain," Edutopia, 2010.

Neuroscientists have been chorusing "cells that fire together, wire together" since the late 1990s, meaning that if you perform a task or recall some information that causes certain neurons to fire in concert, it strengthens the connections between the cells. Over time these connections become thick, hardy road maps that link various parts of the brain, and stimulating one neuron in the sequence is more likely to trigger the next one to fire.

Practice creates permanence. The more the neural network is stimulated, the stronger and more efficient it becomes. In my understanding, this is the essence of the need for repetition in learning so as to create new habits. To me repetition is the principal component of discipline, one of the Three Graces we receive from the universe. If you were once very good at riding bicycles, but stopped doing so a long time ago, you will probably catch up easily when you try again. Not so if you never got to expediency. In that case, you will likely have to start from scratch. If you catch up easily, you will probably feel as if your knowledge was secretly embedded in some part of your body.

John Assaraf, who has also been studying the developments in neuroscience during the last decades, wrote in one of his blogs:

"The fact that your brain is constantly changing and creating new neurons and neural connections based on your environment, predominant thoughts, and experiences means that you can literally and deliberately retrain your own brain. The old adage that 'You cannot teach an old dog new tricks,' has fallen by the wayside and the truth and fact now is that not only can you teach that 'Old Dog' new tricks, but that old dog can release whatever has held him or her back

from reaching their true potential easier and faster than ever before. This we refer to as conscious and deliberate evolution." [68]

Assaraf's greatest interest is in how you and I can take responsibility for our lives and learn what we need to learn in order to become as successful as we want to in our areas of interest. He shows that you can develop your own brain to achieve your purpose. Quoting the same blog, Assaraf makes the following announcements:

"The Challenging News:
- *Your brain is designed to protect you from harm and doesn't like change.*
- *Conscious and unconscious fears are responded to swiftly with a flight, freeze or fight response (this can be good or challenging, depending on the reality of your circumstances).*
- *Unless challenged on an ongoing basis, your brain will do just what it is currently programmed to think and do, and nothing more.*
- *If you don't use it . . . you'll lose it. Basically, the lazier you are, the lazier it is.*

The Good News:
- *Your brain is able to grow new connections, beliefs, and habits while performing at higher levels.*
- *Your brain is your servant and requires your guidance in what you want it to do.*

---

68. http://johnassaraf.com/can-brain-science-really-make-you-happier-wealthier-and-more-successful

- *Your brain can and does perform the most complicated tasks at an unconscious level.*
- *You can retrain your brain to keep you happier, healthier, and wealthier.*
- *You are never too old to take control of your brain and make it more powerful."*

I invite you to enjoy the good news and proceed with the notion that your glass is half full. Your mood will improve and you will be enthusiastic about what is still to come. You now know that your biology allows you to become fulfilled by becoming aware, taking responsibility, and doing some work, like repeating while learning.

In the past few years it has become clear that the human brain can make new neurons starting in your twenties and continuing well into old age. So you can literally rewire your brain with new parts as the older parts wear out.[69] Below are some simple things you can do to preserve, protect, and enhance your nerve cells. They will produce the required effects if exercised consistently. You will need to ask for your Three Graces to be present and operative: Will, Attention, and Discipline (and repetition, right?). Let's take a look at what you can do to have a responding, healthy brain:

- Physical exercise
- Lifelong learning
- Cognitive stimulation (do you like solving puzzles, learning languages?)

---

69. http://www.emedexpert.com/tips/brain.shtml

- Social interactions
- Sleep and naps
- Stress management (relaxation, seeing problems as opportunities)
- Laughter and humor
- Healthy eating habits (don't skip breakfast, eat blueberries)
- Healthy drinking habits (if you drink spirits, choose red wine)
- Regular meditation (I added this one due to my appreciation of how beneficial it is for me to start the day with meditation.)

The Neuroscience of Conversations

We have already seen that conversations and the use of human language best distinguish people from other mammals. A conversation consists not only of verbal language; it also involves the whole body, feelings, emotions, and moods. The body is supported in its vital functions by the reptilian brain, just as other animals' bodies are. Emotional expression is controlled by the limbic system, also an old brain, and not different from the rest of the mammal brain. The great difference lies in our verbal capacity, which resides in the neocortex, and the huge number of connections among all the different structures called neural pathways.

Every conversation affects the three brains and also the neural pathways. Conversations trigger the production of hormones and neurotransmitters, and they also create electrical currents. Research has found that when a conversation produces fear or distrust, or when you read a negative word or have a negative thought, there is a substantial increase of activity in the amygdala. Dozens of stress-producing hormones and neurotransmitters are released, and they interrupt the normal functioning of your brain. Logic, reason, language processing, and communication functions are particularly affected. The more you stay focused in this negativity, the more you can actually damage your memory, feelings, and moods. You might disrupt your sleep, your appetite, and the way your brain regulates happiness, longevity, and health. Furthermore, when you express a negative word, not only your brain is affected, but also your listeners' brains. Everyone experiences increased anxiety and irritability, creating distrust, and therefore undermining the ability to build empathy and cooperation. The brain does not distinguish between fantasy and fact, so every negative input is assumed to be a real danger.

Waldman, a psychologist who, as you have already seen, claims to be a translator of neuroscientific findings for the general public, and Andrew Newberg, a medical doctor, tell us that it is possible to retrain your brain by interrupting the negative thoughts and fears.[70] By redirecting awareness to setting positive goals and building a strong, optimistic sense of accomplishment, you strengthen the areas in the frontal lobe that suppress your tendency to react to imaginary fears.

---

70. A. Newberg and M. Waldman, *Words Can Change Your Brain*, Penguin Group (USA), 2012.

- Is it possible to overcome instincts we share with other animals through awareness and learning?
- How easy is it to change your brain voluntarily? What would you do if you wanted to change it?

The anthropologist, coach, and consultant Judith Glaserdeveloped a model she calls The Conversational Dashboard™.[71] It is a visual representation of what happens in the brain during conversations. She defined "protect" behaviors and "partner" behaviors. The primitive brain, where fear and distrust reside, deals with protect behaviors, and the prefrontal cortex relates to partner behaviors, which involve more advanced human capacities such as trust, integrity, strategic thinking, and regulating emotions. A threatening situation floods our brain with the neurotransmitter cortisol, which closes off the higher functions, making them inaccessible even if the intention is there.

If you have acquired conversational skills, and use them well, the hormone oxytocin, among other neurotransmitters, is released. This chemical can create comforting feelings of well-being. Glaser tells us that this hormone's power might explain why loners die young and why emotional rejection can be more painful than physical trauma.

Glaser explains that human beings have conversational blind spots that prevent us from connecting mind to mind with others and allow for conflicts and breakdowns. She identified the following general blind spots, with their corresponding brain activites:

---
71. Judith E. Glaser, *Conversational Intelligence*, Bibliomotion Inc., 2014.

1. *Persuade others we are right.*

    The dopamine (yet another neurotransmitter) level rises.

    Winning a point might make you feel good—and others bad—but you often do not realize that.

2. *Failure to realize that fear, trust, and distrust change how we see and interpret reality, and therefore how we talk about it.*

    The release of cortisol and catecholamine closes down the prefrontal cortex.

    We do not realize that we move into protective behaviors.

3. *Inability to stand in each other's shoes when we are fearful or upset. (I call this lack of empathy.)*

    We disconnect the mirror nervous system (discovered by Giacomo Rizolatti in 1999[72]) that gives us a view into what others feel, think, and intend.

    Our sensitivity to others' perspectives recedes.

4. *Assumption of remembering what others say.*

    Because of our internal process and the chemicals produced, we remember what we think others said.

    Our internal listening and dialogue trump the other person's speech. (You saw this in chapter 12.)

---

72. http://www.gocognitive.net/interviews/giacomo-rizzolatti-mirror-neurons

5. *Assumption that meaning resides in the speaker.*

   If you are the listener, your brain pulls the meaning of what you are hearing from your experiences, specifically from the hippocampus, where memory is stored in the limbic system. Then you bring the memory of these experiences into the conversation to make sense of what you listened to.

   As said in chapter 12, meaning resides in the listener until the speaker validates that what was listened to and what was spoken match.

   - See if you can identify one or more blind spots in yourself.
   - If yes, what action can you take to overcome each one?

Neuroscience beyond the Cephalic Brain: Your Heart and Gut

It is possible to trace the first scientific knowledge of the brain to the mid-sixteenth century during the Renaissance.[73] Until then people believed that the heart was the center of a person's emotions. Several years later, during the seventeenth century, two scientists who were also philosophers debated whether reasoning or feeling was more important in human life. Descartes, whom we learned of earlier in this chapter,

---
73. https://faculty.washington.edu/chudler/hist.html

stated, "I think, hence I am,"[74] whereas for Blaise Pascal, "The heart has its reasons which reason knows not."[75]

- To whose statement is your heart closer: Descartes's or Pascal's? Explain the reason for your answer.
- To whose statement is your gut closer? Explain the reason for your answer.
- Which of the two questions was easier for you to answer? Explain the reason.

Twenty-first-century advances in neuroscience provide hard evidence that the brain, heart, and gut are biologically connected. These findings are quite recent and it is not possible to expect that everyone has been updated. Nevertheless people tend to accept the importance of the connection of the gut and heart to the brain however biologically unknown it is to them. The following quotes illustrate what I am stating:

"A good head and a good heart are always a formidable combination."[76]
Nelson Mandela, South African and world leader

"Trust your gut feeling about things, listen to what others are saying, and look at the results of your actions. Once you know the

---

74. http://www.bartleby.com/34/1/4.html
75. https://www.goodreads.com/quotes/5635-the-heart-has-its-reasons-which-reason-knows-not
76. http://www.brainyquote.com/quotes/quotes/n/nelsonmand101682.html?src=t_heart

truth, you can set about taking action to improve. Everyone will be better for it."[77]

Jack Canfield, author and coaching guru

"I wouldn't dream of working on something that didn't make my gut rumble and my heart want to explode!"[78]

Kate Winslet, actress

- What is your interpretation of each of these quotes?
- Find an experience in your life in which you could have used each one, or in which you expected or desired future experiences to which each one is relevant.

Neuroscientific research concerning the brain, gut, and heart connections is newer than the already challenging cephalic brain research. Notwithstanding, there is sufficient evidence collected so far to state that there are three brains in the body, located in the head (the brain), the center of the body (the heart), and the belly (most of the digestive system from pylorus to anus). They are called cephalic,cardiac, and enteric brains.

Many years ago I was taught in school that the heart is an organ that pumps blood throughout the body via the circulatory system, supplying oxygen and nutrients to the tissues and removing carbon dioxide and other wastes. Probably this is what you were taught, as are today's schoolchildren. I think that in one or two more generations schools will teach the same plus add in the neural function of the heart.

---

77. http://www.brainyquote.com/quotes/quotes/j/jackcanfie637620.html?src=t_gut
78. http://www.brainyquote.com/quotes/quotes/k/katewinsle386847.html?src=t_gut

The same can be said about the gut (small intestine and colon). It is an important part of a complex system in charge of absorbing nutrients and minerals from ingested food (small intestine) and concentrating, storing, and preparing for excretion of solid refuse.

The gut has been called the "second brain" for many years.[79] Actually it arises from the same tissues as the central nervous system (cephalic brain) during fetal development in the mother's womb. Therefore it has many structural and chemical parallels to the brain. The second brain does not need to receive information from the cephalic brain to fulfill its role, although they communicate actively. The principal connection between the gut and the cephalic brain is through the vagus nerve, which also connects with the heart.

As an example of the importance of the gut in neural activity, it has been found that the majority of the body's serotonin, between 80 and 90%, is produced in the gastrointestinal tract. Serotonin that is used in the cephalic brain must be produced within it. It is thought that serotonin can affect mood, social behavior, appetite, digestion, sleep, memory, sexual desire, and sexual function.

Grant Soosalu and Marvin Oka[80] created a method for changing behavior from these findings.[81] They think that one day multiple brains will have been discovered beyond the three that have been indicated here. Soosalu and Oka state that just as

---
79. https://www.ncbi.nlm.nih.gov/pmc/articles/PMC3845678/
80. http://www.mbraining.com/
81. G. Soosalu and M. Oka, *mBraining*, copyright mBit, 2012.

the brain in the head does, the gut brain and the heart brain can think, store information (creating memory), learn, and adapt.

The cephalic brain, consisting of the reptilian, limbic, and neocortex systems, has fifty to 100 billion neurons. The enteric or second brain has 200 to 500 million neurons, and the cardiac brain has thirty to 120 thousand neurons.

With this degree of neural structure and connectivity, and the recursive capacity for human learning that our language provides, it is difficult to imagine what level of sophisticated development humanity will reach. It is crucial to watch closely the alignment of all the brains. The world needs all the scientists, engineers, technology innovators, medical doctors, consultants, psychologists, and coaches it can generate. Multidisciplinary teams are needed to coordinate efforts in discovering more about who we are, how we are made, and what is our level of freedom for change and human design. Humankind is responsible for providing conditions of a good life for itself.

Keep an eye on present and future neuroscientific discoveries. Awareness of how the brain works and the changes it can produce in who we are will become a key tool for designing and travelling a path for fulfillment.

CHAPTER 18

The Novel Entrepreneur

This book has now come to an end. In it you found strategies, methods, tools, stories, questions, exercises, and knowledge ranging from philosophy to experiential knowledge to neuroscience. This knowledge is all meant to help you find your way to design, build, and travel your heart-centered path for fulfillment.

The term *entrepreneurship* has been traditionally used in the area of business. This might be so because the person who coined the term was the French economist Jean Baptiste Say. He was very impressed by Adam Smith's *The Wealth of Nations,* a book that every student of economics in the world must be acquainted with to this day. But for Say there was a character missing in Smith's book. Say named this character "entrepreneur," which might be literally translated from the French language as "adventurer." An entrepreneur is a person who recognizes opportunities and manages them effectively.[82] As a cotton manufacturer, Say considered himself an entrepreneur and thought that entrepreneurship must be included in business literature.

The Merriam-Webster dictionary lists the traditional meaning of entrepreneur: "Someone who assumes, organizes, and manages the risks of a business or enterprise." Say would likely agree with this definition that is used today by many people, companies, and academia.

Take a look now at the following definition provided by Dictionary.com: "a person who organizes and manages any enterprise, especially a business, usually with considerable initiative and risk." The word *any* is not trivial in this definition. It suggests that entrepreneurs are those who identify a need—any need—and fill it. The need is felt as an urge, and it can be wealth creation, community problem-solving, providing good working conditions, improving the quality of life on the planet, or any other need.

> Assuming you think of yourself as an entrepreneur, or you want to become one:
> - Are you an entrepreneur?
> - If the answer is yes, what makes you one?
> - If the answer is no, what is missing?
> - What is the need you want to satisfy?

---

82. http://www.investopedia.com/ask/answers/08/origin-of-entrepreneur.asp

- What actions will turn you into an entrepreneur or a more accomplished one?

The novel entrepreneur's starting point is the calling or the urge to satisfy a need. They imagine, dream, and talk to themselves and to others until they formulate a world-changing declaration. They call this declaration their vision. From then on they hold the necessary conversations and take the necessary actions that allow them to develop their venture.

The novel entrepreneur probably owns or leads an organization at some point in their career. Nevertheless you do not need to be a business owner in order to be an entrepreneur. In fact some experts claim that by about 2030 everyone will have to be an entrepreneur,[83] including corporation employees.

Howard Schultz is an entrepreneur who was already one when he persuaded the founders of coffee house Starbucks to hire him as a marketing director. Schultz became an employed entrepreneur. In 1983, he was sent to an international housewares show in Milan. While walking around the city he encountered several espresso bars where owners knew their customers by name and served drinks like cappuccinos and cafe lattes. He went back home with the recipes of those drinks and tripled Starbucks's sales over the next year. However, the concept of the Italian café amazed Schultz the most. It was not just a store but a place for social meetings and leisure.[84] The more

---

83. https://www.entrepreneur.com/article/228176
84. "Howard Schultz Biography: Success Story of Starbucks CEO." Astrum People, (2016). Web. 12 May 2016.

traditional owners would not accept this vision and did not agree to change the concept. Schultz decided to create his own company in 1985. In 1987 he bought Starbucks, becoming its president and CEO. Starbucks is a global company that in 2016 had 191 thousand employees worldwide and annual sales of more than $16 billion, and Schultz's personal fortune is estimated to be $3 billion.

Schultz was born to a lower-middle-class family. One day his father broke an ankle and could not work as a diaper deliveryman for quite some time. This meant he did not receive a salary, and the whole family had to live in miserable conditions. This event deeply impressed Schultz, who in my interpretation became an entrepreneur and later a billionaire to honor his father by reversing the family's financial situation. This was the need he felt an urgency to address. In his book *Pour Your Heart into It* he revealed that his tremendous professional success is a tribute to his late father, who "never attained fulfillment and dignity from work he found meaningful."[85]

In the book Schultz shows what his key success factors in building a stellar company are. I consider the following three the most outstanding: a passion for making great coffee a part of the American experience, making employees' well-being his first priority, and maintaining the quality of the product.

Schultz balanced his inner quest with his desire to change some aspect of the outer world. This is the essence of a heart-centered entrepreneur. Actually the book title *Pour Your Heart into It* comes as no surprise to me either.

---
85. H. Schultz and D. J. Yang, *Pour Your Heart Into It*, Hyperion, 1997.

A novel entrepreneur always looks to themselves and to the outer world, and aligns their sense of the needs "out there" with their sense of identity and the dreams they have for themselves and the world. They have an ambition to turn their dreams into reality. That mood is a driving force to take action. They know that life will not always be pleasant and comfortable since they will always be learning. And learning usually drives people out of their comfort zones. If they fail, they accept it and keep going responsibly, without victimizing themselves. They know that they need to persevere. And they are often afraid, in spite of which they move forward, which prevents them from fearing fear.

A novel entrepreneur becomes a leader. They start by creating their own path for fulfillment while developing their leadership style. Their passion and love for life and people drive them to succeed. They not only trust their thinking head but also their heart and gut. And they use all the tools that they constantly receive during their journey.

Are you ready to dive into your path for fulfillment?

ACKNOWLEDGMENTS

This is delicious! Feeling a sense of deep gratitude is one of my most cherished emotions. And the time has come to express this gratitude publicly.

I have many people to thank for this book. I hope that I am fair to all of them. I want to start with my husband, Gustavo Silva Cabello. As usual, he stood by me silently, encouraging and often swallowing his frustration for my lack of availability to him. He was as happy as I was when I told him I had finished writing this book. My success is his success, too. That's how it's been for the last thirty years. Thank you, Gustavo. You taught me how to build my path for fulfillment and never left me alone.

Next I would like to thank my first two coaching masters, Rafael Echeverría, who kindly wrote the foreword for this book, and Julio Olalla. Through them my life turned upside down. They taught me a new and powerful narrative and how to become a good coach. During the process my basic mood in life changed completely. I went from being a highly judgmental and resigned person to becoming very enthusiastic and passionate about the possibilities the universe offers us. Perhaps it is not a coincidence that you came into my life at about the same time as Gustavo.

I thank our children, Jaime, Sebastián, Claudia, and Cathy, for giving me the opportunity to test all possible emotions, for sometimes putting my frontal cortex to the test while they were growing up, and for bringing our beautiful grandchildren to this world. I hope they will read this book one day and find clues for living a good life in an increasingly uncertain world.

I met Christine Kloser several years ago through one of her incredibly generous Transformational Author Experience seminars on the Internet. Later I enrolled in her "Get Your Book Done" program, and was a coauthor of *Pebbles in the Pond (Wave Four)*. The latter gave me the opportunity to meet her in person and declare my admiration face to face. I was so happy to hear that she has her own publishing house now and that I could be her client once again. In practical terms, I doubt that I would have finished this book without the heart-centered path for fulfillment that I travelled with her guiding hand and spirit. Thank you, Christine. You made this book possible.

Marlene Oulton is the first editor of the book. Here is something funny: I don't tend to associate official editors with angels or fairies, and yet this is the case with Marlene. She helped me discover and recover my creative energy. I only know her laughs, smiles, and good will. Nothing but good can come out of this mood. Marlene travelled the journey with me, waving a magic wand.

ACKNOWLEDGEMENTS

My second editor is Michelle Cohen. She definitely helped me improve my style in her quiet, wonderfully professional way. Thank you, Michelle!

Carrie Jareed, Director for Transformation Books Publishing, had, as her mission, to pull me to the ground when I flew too high. Carrie is responsible for keeping my timing within the limits of reality. She has always been present and ready to give me a hand. Thank you, Carrie.

I also want to thank Viki Winterton and her team for helping me announce that a (hopefully) good book was coming.

My friends Susie Fröhlich and Yvonne Mc Manus, and my friend and colleague Lisa Wood, read the first version of the first chapters of my manuscript. They encouraged me to keep on writing and gave me some good ideas to make the book comprehensive for a large audience. Thank you for that, dear friends!

A book needs some density, some kind of texture in order to attract the attention of the reader and to make sense of what it narrates or conveys. That texture is provided by a rather long and exciting life, and, most of all, by professional interactions with thousands of people and hundreds of clients. They inspired me to invent the stories you read in this book and they are also the reason I continue travelling the coaching, leadership, and writing path. Thank you, dear clients!

And last but not least, I thank you, my reader. I wrote this book for you. Please connect with me at www.thenovelentrepreneur.com.

Thank you, thank you, and thank you!

ABOUT THE AUTHOR

Sally Bendersky is the grandmother of seven. She is also a chemical engineer, systems analyst, gestalt therapist, and certified professional coach. She integrated her training background through working with individuals and organizations in several fields of action. She took leadership roles in her positions as ambassador of Chile in Israel, executive director of a technology development center, and Secretary of Higher Education in Chile.

Sally also exercised leadership in the field of coaching, producing and managing the first international coaching certification in Spanish, in 1992. She created two international courses for improving certified coaches' skills and helped hundreds of managers develop strategies and leadership in their organizations.

Since 2016, Sally has been president of the board of directors of the Port of Coquimbo in Chile. She also presides a Consulting Committee for innovation and entrepreneurship at the faculty of engineering of her alma mater, Universidad de Chile. She is the only woman belonging to the Chilean Academy of Engineering.

Sally is a coauthor of two bestselling books: *Pebbles in the Pond, Wave Four,* edited by Christine Kloser, and *Confidence: Volume One,* edited by Ana Rosenberg.

Sally founded New Leadership, a company that aims to create a global movement of integrated leadership for co-creating new practices in organizations that include the talents of all their members, so that productivity and well-being will turn into realities throughout the world.

www.thenovelentrepreneur.com

www.ingramcontent.com/pod-product-compliance
Lightning Source LLC
Chambersburg PA
CBHW071602080526
44588CB00010B/992